Do Your Own
HOME PLUMBING

DO YOUR OWN
HOME PLUMBING

HAROLD KING

London
W. FOULSHAM & CO LTD
New York · Toronto · Capetown · Sydney

W. FOULSHAM & CO LTD
Yeovil Road, Slough, Bucks, England

ISBN 0 572 00830 9

Designed by Rosemary Harley
Photoset and Printed in Great Britain by
Redwood Press Limited, Trowbridge, Wiltshire

CONTENTS

1

PLANNING YOUR PLUMBING

Modern domestic plumbing is no longer the expression of a complex set of skills, involving the rigmarole of clumsy petrol or paraffin blow lamps, the need to acquire the arts of lead burning, and the ability to use taps and dies to join heavy, galvanized pipe. Nowadays there is a greater sophistication in approach, and developments both in materials and in the techniques of using them make plumbing work very much simpler. Copper, stainless steel and a variety of plastic materials are now in wide use, and unlike some of the older ones these materials do not tend to fur up or rust. Modern plumbing is not only much quicker to install, but neater and more efficient.

While developments and refinements in plumbing have been considerable in recent years, the Romans had developed a sophisticated system of plumbing some 2000 years ago, using ducts to distribute water. By the Middle Ages, however, plumbing had become so primitive that disease was rife, reminding us now that sewage and waste disposal are aspects of plumbing vital to the health of the community.

Plumbing falls into two general categories: domestic or indoor plumbing, providing fresh water at the kitchen tap and storage, both hot and cold, for washing and ancillary purposes; and sewage and waste disposal, which one might broadly call drains. Another aspect of plumbing is storm-water drainage.

Firstly, how much water do we consume? In an average modern town, people use an estimated 910 litres (200 gallons) a day. A bath takes around 91 litres (20 gallons), washing 23 litres (five gallons), and even the washing of hands accounts for seven litres ($1\frac{1}{2}$ gallons). Taking into consideration the amount of water used by industry, we arrive at a staggering consumption of thousands of millions of litres a day. It follows that plumbing services should be well installed and not lead to waste. Such things as faulty overflows and dripping taps can, cumulatively, lead to great losses of water.

Many homes still possess ancient festoons of indoor pipe-work forming an ugly clutter around walls, and all too often in a state of growing deterioration. Frequently this plumbing offers limited facilities. Updating the plumbing may, at the same time, suggest improvements in the layouts of kitchens and bathrooms. Where, for example, hot water is furnished by a small boiler, which does not provide any degree of space heating, the opportunity may well be taken to bring the heating system up to date, since if a domestic hot-water circulating system is fitted, this may be taken in hand at the same time as domestic replumbing.

Initially, one should make a careful assessment of the present and future plumbing needs of the home. It is important to look ahead, since adaptations made later are often more expensive, time-consuming and frequently less satisfactory. Consider how your needs fit in with the updating of arrangements in the kitchen and bathroom. Perhaps the kitchen could be fitted with labour-saving devices, such as a washing machine, water heater, waste-disposal unit, or dishwasher. In the bathroom provision could be made for a water heater, shower or bidet. Often, it is an opportunity to consider fitting a new toilet suite and bath. There are advantages in providing extra toilet facilities in the downstairs part of the house; a store or lobby may be suitable for conversion, but where a WC is adjacent to a kitchen a lobby and an extra door may be required. Another improvement is to fit one of the special toilet extractor fans, which operate at a slower and then a faster speed before switching themselves off.

It is always necessary to inform the local authority of any major replumbing plans, though this is not necessary where, for example, a cracked basin or WC pan has to be changed. Permission is basically needed for major alterations, such as re-routing of pipework and redesigning of the general layout.

A plan should be made of what is proposed and submitted to the local authority for approval. It should show all the detail, even stopcocks and valves, in addition to all proposed changes in circuitry. You should also show the existing layout for comparison. For a bungalow, a simple plan drawing is sufficient; for a house, the full elevations should be shown. These need not be drawn to full architectural standards—and you should find that local officials are most helpful in offering guidance as to the requirements and will be ready to give advice on the sketch plans.

It is also necessary to comply with the by-laws of the local water authority, and a copy of these should first be studied. This will help to ensure that your plans meet the approval of all parties without the need to make frustrating changes in your proposals.

Some improvements can qualify for discretionary grants from the local council—for example a toilet, new bath or shower system. For a new bath or shower one can normally obtain a grant of up to £200. Work which does not qualify for grants can, of course, be linked with work which does.

It is not always appreciated that grants can be obtained for work carried out on a do-it-yourself basis; in this case they are only for materials—labour cannot be charged. Grants are made on a pound-for-pound basis, up to the limit of £1,000. Your local authority can provide more details.

Once you have designed your new plumbing system and obtained any necessary approval, think out your course of action. Always work to a definite plan; map out a programme for the job. Particularly, make sure that the household is not robbed of water supplies for any lengthy period. Try to work in stages and plumb in as much of the service in advance before connecting this in, in order to leave the exisitng services in operation for as long as possible.

Work out carefully all the materials needed—and then make a double check, particularly if you are carrying out work over a weekend. It can be disastrous to have the domestic plumbing out of action for the lack of the odd component or fitting just because the suppliers have shut!

How many WCs and wash basins do you need in your home? While individual requirements may vary, minimum standards are recommended in a Government publication entitled *Homes for Today and Tomorrow*. These are: one WC (in bathroom) to serve one to three persons in a household; one WC (separate) to serve four-person households in a one-, two- or three-storey house or two-storey maisonette, also five-person households in flats and single-storey houses; two WCs (one in the bathroom) to serve five-person households in two- or three-storey homes, two-storey maisonettes and households of six persons in flats or single-storey homes. In cases where a separate WC does not adjoin a bathroom, it must contain a wash basin. The diagrams show the space which is required for reasonable access to individual fittings. The bathroom layout for the best utilization of a limited space, from the HMSO publication *Space in the Home,* shows a room measuring 2.47 m × 1.37 m (9 ft × 4 ft 6 in). A sliding door divides the wash basin from the bath and WC. This allows privacy for two people in the bathroom at the same time. The window is best placed over the basin, and a high-level window, or one with 'modesty glass', is suggested over the bath. If the sliding door were omitted, the window over the bath could be dispensed with, since sufficient light would enter from the other. The linen cupboard is a desirable optional extra.

MATERIALS AND METHODS

Before you tackle any main domestic plumbing it is really necessary to know something about the methods of cutting, manipulating and jointing various types of pipe, and about fittings and how to use them. The materials in most general use are copper, stainless steel and various plastics, including glass-reinforced plastics (GRP), or glass fibre, as it is better known. The choice of materials is always an individual one. Copper has taken over from lead and galvanized mild steel as the conventional material for main plumbing circuitry. Plastics, however, are rapidly gaining ground and can be simpler and cheaper to fit than traditional metal plumbing.

It is also important to look at the various tools and equipment which can speed up work and ensure efficient connections. Remember, leaking services can rapidly cause many hundreds of pounds' worth of damage, once a flood breaks loose!

Let us start by looking at the use of metal pipe and fittings and the tools you need for general plumbing work, and then consider the use of plastic services, either on their own or linked with copper or stainless-steel pipework. It may be necessary, in some cases, to connect lead to certain of these materials and this will be discussed later in the book.

HACKSAWS AND ROTARY CUTTERS

Pipes are cut with a hacksaw or a rotary pipe cutter. The standard hacksaw is either 254 mm (10 in) or 305 mm (12 in) long. Some hacksaws can be adjusted to either dimension. A junior hacksaw is often useful, since it can cut in awkward places more readily than its larger counterpart.

For cutting soft copper, low-tungsten steel blades can be used. With stainless steel, the more expensive but more durable high-speed steel blades are needed. For pipe over 15 mm

($\frac{1}{4}$ in) in diameter a blade with 22 teeth to 25 mm (1 in) should be used.

Blades should be fitted with the teeth pointing away from the handle; there will usually be an arrow on the blade to indicate the direction of fitting. Adjust the wingnut to take up the slack in the blade and then apply just three full turns.

When cutting with a hacksaw, the pipe should be firmly secured. Use a long, steady stroke at a rate of about one per second for low-tungsten blades and about seventy per minute for high-speed steel, releasing pressure on the return stroke. Do not start a new blade in an old cut. Support the pipe adequately on either side, so as to avoid distortion when cutting. Use a cloth to wipe off swarf and never the hand. The foot can be used as an improvised support. If you are right-handed, you can support the pipe on top of your left foot.

The rotary pipe cutter cuts both fast and accurately. If any amount of pipe cutting is necessary, one is a sound investment. It is adjustable to various sizes of pipe and possesses two toughened wheels and a cutter, mounted on a frame to form a triangle. One has a threaded spindle which gives adjustment to fit the pipe. Cutting is achieved by rotating the unit, gradually tightening the spindle to deepen the cut until the pipe is severed.

FILES

You may need both a flat and a round file. This largely depends on whether you are using a hacksaw or a rotary pipe cutter. The pipe cutter has a device at one end to remove burrs from the pipe, which would otherwise cause turbulence and impede the flow of water. The round file is used to take the burrs from inside the mouth of the pipe where a cut has been made using a hacksaw.

Also where a hacksaw is employed, the flat file is afterwards used across the face of the cut, to remove any irregularities and also to chamfer the outer pipe ends slightly, to make the connection of fittings easier. The pipe cutter puts a slight bevel on the cut, and this procedure is therefore not necessary.

12

SPANNERS

Two adjustable spanners are needed where compression fittings are used. The most suitable size is either 254 mm (10 in) or 305 mm (12 in) long. If you have to remove heavily rusted iron fittings, a pair of Stillson-pattern wrenches may be needed.

BENDING SPRINGS AND PIPE BENDERS

Bending springs, or a bending machine, which can be bought or hired, are the best means of bending pipe. In any event 15 mm ($\frac{1}{2}$ in) elbow fittings should be used sparingly as turbulence and resistance can result at such joints.

Bending springs must be appropriate to the gauge and also, of course, correspond with the bore of the pipe, which will be either 15 mm or 22 mm ($\frac{1}{2}$ in or $\frac{3}{4}$ in). A bending spring consists of a piece of tough coiled spring steel which is inserted into the pipe at the position of the required bend—this should fall roughly in the middle of the length of pipe.

There is an eye at the top of the spring, and a piece of flexible wire or nylon should be attached to this to facilitate the removal of the spring from the pipe. The eye can also be used to help remove a tight spring by inserting a screwdriver through this and turning it to 'unscrew' the spring.

Bending is achieved by an even pressure of the pipe against the knee, under the kneecap. If you slightly overbend the pipe and then unbend it a little, the spring should be easy to remove. However, it is best to underbend a pipe and then check the angle, since a greatly overbent pipe is difficult to correct.

A useful device you can make is an extension bar. This is designed to eliminate waste of tube when using a bending spring. Without one it is difficult to obtain a short end of less than 150 mm or 200 mm because anything less leaves very little handhold; thus, where a short tail is required up to 150 mm of tube is wasted.

You need a 300 mm length of tube of the same diameter as that being worked and a straight connector compression fitting, from which you file out the central ridge or stop inside.

13

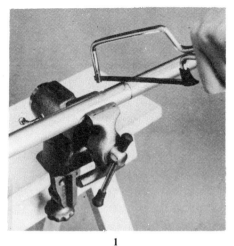
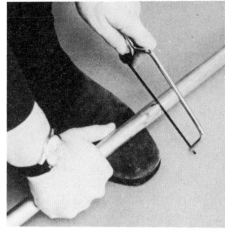

1

2

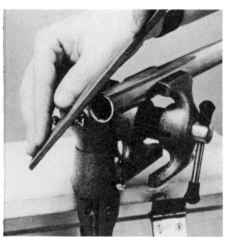

3

4

1. Junior hacksaw is the best general-purpose tool for cutting tube

2. Foot can be used as a support for the tube where vice is not available

3. Flat file used to chamfer end of tube and remove external burrs

4. Burrs inside tube are removed with a round file

5. Rotary pipe cutter makes a clean cut

6. Bending spring is slid into the tube

7. Tube is then bent across the knee by hand pressure on each side

8. Improvised bar facilitates removal of spring; this may be of almost any material

9. Pipe-bending machine speeds up work where there is any quantity of bending to be done

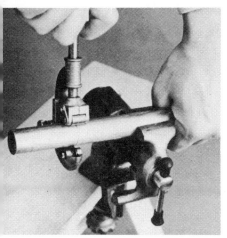
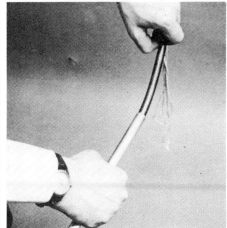

5

6

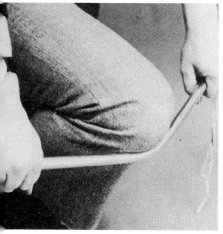

7

8

9

The fitting is then securely attached to one end of the 300 mm tube.

This extension bar enables a bend with a tail of only 75 mm to 100 mm to be made. To use it, slide the spring through the bar and fitting and then into the tube which is to be bent. Lightly tighten the loose end of the straight connector and it will be rigid enough to make the small-tailed bend.

LIGHTWEIGHT VICE

A lightweight portable engineering vice with fibre jaws, or a pipe vice, is a good investment. You can hold lengths of pipe in its jaws without damage during cutting. Never overtighten the jaws of the vice as you may distort the pipe.

BLOW TORCH

A blow torch—the butane-gas pattern is cheap and satisfactory—will be needed for any solder-jointing work. There are two types: those with an exchange cannister, for which you obtain a refill, and the throw-away cannister, for which you buy a replacement. More professional blow torches have large cannisters, connected to the torch head by flexible pipe. These are the best investment if you have any fair amount of plumbing and soldering work to do.

COPPER AND STAINLESS-STEEL TUBE

The copper tube now used in plumbing is of the light-gauge hard-temper type, known as Table III tube. Any bending springs used have to correspond with this gauge. The older, thicker Table I tube, though of the same gauge, can only be

10. Typical unequal compression tee junction

11. Compression return tee fitting with slow bend

12. Corner tee compression fitting

13. A corner cross fitting

14. Slow bend with drain cock, compression-ended

15. Compression-ended stop cock with drain-off tap

10

11

12

13

14

15

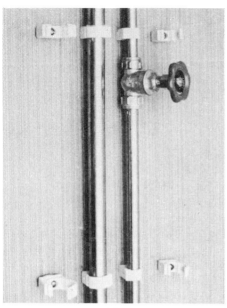

17

16

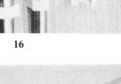

18   19

16. Gate valve, compression-ended, in run of tube. Note plastic pipe clips

17. Components making up a reducing set for compression fitting

18. Typical compression straight coupling

19. Similar fittings, capillary and compression-ended, equal-tee junctions

bent only with a Table I spring. Table III springs are also needed for stainless-steel tube. Copper and stainless steel are the two most common materials used in plumbing. Copper is easier than stainless steel to cut and bend. The price of copper fluctuates rather more than that of stainless steel, and prevailing prices may determine which you choose.

OTHER PIPEWORK

Lead and galvanized-steel pipework is found in older houses and it usually pays to remove this and replace it with the neater modern pipework, especially since older pipework may be heavily furred and so impede water flow. Moreover, special techniques and connectors may be needed to join up old lead and barrel pipe to modern services, and the results may not be altogether satisfactory. For example, connecting galvanized pipe to copper can lead to corrosion problems, particularly in hard-water areas, where there is a danger of electrolytic corrosion occurring as a result of joining these two metals. A special fitting is needed to separate these if they are used together.

When dismantling pipework, a pair of Stillson-pattern wrenches are needed to loosen rusted joints. These wrenches enable you to clamp a section of pipe with one of them while manipulating that which is joined to it with the other. Heat or penetrating oil may be needed to remove stubborn fittings, but heat will only be effective where water has been fully drained from the pipes.

Steel barrel pipework is still used for some services but requires the use of stocks and dies in order to join sections together. A set of stocks and dies is relatively expensive to buy but can usually be obtained from one of the various hire sources. This pipe is relatively cheap, compared with copper or stainless steel, and is sometimes used for gas service to domestic appliances.

You need a firm bench, with a heavily anchored pipe vice. It also requires a fair amount of physical strength to cut threads on pipe. A metal lubricant should be used to ease the

19

cutting operation.

Joints can be sealed by hemp 'teased' into a thin string and smeared lightly with a plumbing compound, or with ptfe tape which is merely wrapped around the pipe in the direction of the thread, leaving the first thread or so clear. Hemp is not encouraged by the authorities for pipe used to supply gas.

It is questionable whether the lower price, set against hire costs for stocks and dies and the effort involved, really warrants the use of barrel pipe instead of copper, stainless steel or plastic.

FITTINGS

The two basic types of fitting are the capillary and the compression fitting. There are two types of both: in compression, the manipulative and the non-manipulative; in capillary, the solder and the solderless, or end-feed type.

Fittings come in a variety of sizes and types. The most common are elbows, tee-pieces, and straight connectors. In addition, there are 'tap' connectors designed for fitting to male-iron threads such as taps and ball valves, connectors with flanged surfaces to fit storage cisterns and drain cocks, stop ends, blank ends, and more unusual fittings such as swept tees and 'obtuse' bends.

Where 15 mm or $\frac{1}{2}$ in fittings are required, a better, lower-turbulence water flow is achieved by 'slow' bends, rather than by use of 'tight' bends.

Compression fittings

The manipulative fitting is seldom used for domestic plumbing. It is used largely for connection of such services as central-heating oil pipelines. A special tool is needed to 'bell' the mouth of the pipe which compresses against the fitting to make the joint.

Non-manipulative fittings utilize a brass or copper cone or olive which tightens around the pipe to make the joint. These cones can be consolidated with a smear of a proprietary non-toxic plumbing compound. This is not essential but helps to ensure a watertight joint.

20

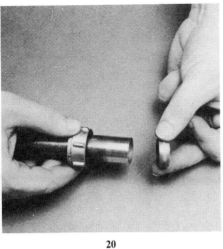
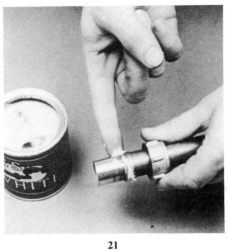

20   **21**

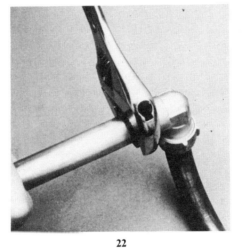

22

Stages in assembling a compression-ended fitting

20. Olive ring slides on to tube after lock nut is positioned

21. A smear of non-toxic plumbing compound is applied to the olive

22. Spanner is used to compress olive on to flange in mouth of fitting; avoid excessive tightening

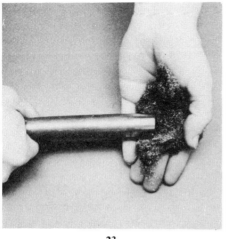

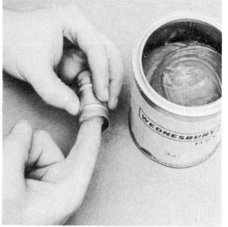

23

24

25

26

Stages in making a solder joint

23. Clean pipe thoroughly using wire wool.

24. Inside of fitting is similarly cleaned and flux is applied to this and to tube

25. Heat is applied evenly in order to melt solder inside rim of fitting

26. Finished solder joint. Note rim of solder around the mouth

27. End-feed solder fitting. Solder is induced into mouth of fitting

28. Reducing set used with solder fitting. This is simply a fitting within a fitting, using same techniques in preparation and soldering

29. Plumbing compound applied to threaded jump prior to hemp seal

30. Hemp is 'teased' into a strand and wrapped around the thread.

31,32. Ptfe tape is a more modern way of sealing and lubricating threaded joints

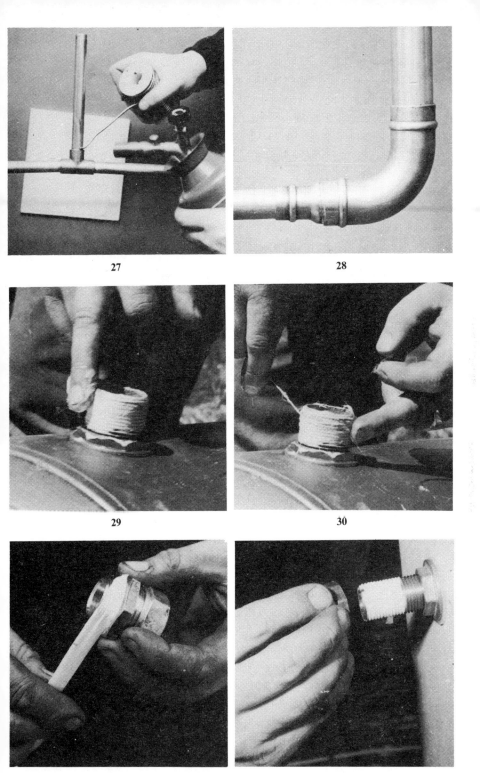

27

28

29

30

31

32

Once the pipes are engaged in the mouth of the fitting, the nuts should be hand tightened, taking care to ensure that the pipes do not creep out. They should be pushed well home. Two or three turns with the spanner, once the nuts are hand tightened, should be adequate. Always take care not to over-tighten the nuts, or you may strip the thread, or the olive may be deeply dented into the pipe, giving a bad union.

Capillary fittings

Capillary fittings are both cheaper and less bulky than compression fittings but the joints need rather more skill to make.

Before making a capillary joint, the pipe and the inside of the fitting must be thoroughly cleaned, using fine wire wool. The inside of the fitting and the pipe should next be coated lightly with flux and the pipe twisted in, to distribute the flux. Excess is wiped off the joint.

Apply heat evenly to the fitting with the blow torch until a ring of solder appears around the mouth of the fitting. A touch of solder to the mouth of the hot joint will run an extra consolidating ring around this—though this is simply a precaution. Avoid overheating as this will 'burn' the solder and may lead to a leaking joint.

End-feed fittings contain no solder. The fitting and pipe are prepared as previously and the fitting is heated up evenly. Feed solder evenly into the mouth of the joint until a ring is left around the edge. Once the joint has cooled, wipe off any excess flux.

Stainless-steel pipe can also be solder jointed. However, ordinary flux is not suitable. An 'aggressive' flux, to remove the oxide film which forms quickly on stainless steel, is necessary.

These acid-based fluxes are available in liquid and paste form. They are highly corrosive and should be handled carefully. Excess flux must be removed from the outside of the pipe and the pipe also flushed out.

As the thermal conductivity of stainless steel is less than that for copper, the heat should be directed on to the fitting and not on to the pipe.

PIPE AND FITTING SIZES

The correct way to describe a tee-piece fitting, one with more than two outlets, is to indicate the sizes of the connection in line with each other, followed by the branch-connection size. Thus, for example, an equal 15 mm ($\frac{1}{2}$ in) tee with 22 mm or $\frac{3}{4}$ in branch is a 15 mm × 15 mm × 22 mm or $\frac{1}{2}$ in × $\frac{1}{2}$ in × $\frac{3}{4}$ in tee.

The following are the metric equivalents of imperial-gauge pipe. The outside diameter (OD) is used in metric measurements. This applies to both plastic and metal tube.

$\frac{3}{8}$ in	$\frac{1}{2}$ in	$\frac{3}{4}$ in	1 in	$1\frac{1}{4}$ in	$1\frac{1}{2}$ in	2 in
10 mm	15 mm	22 mm	28 mm	35 mm	42 mm	54 mm

The following sizes are interchangeable without adaptation:

$\frac{3}{8}$ in	10 mm
$\frac{1}{2}$ in	15 mm
1 in	28 mm
2 in	54 mm

25

3

PLASTIC PLUMBING

Plastic pipework and fittings are widely used in plumbing. These weigh substantially less than their counterparts in steel, lead or copper and are simple to fit.

The plastics family is a large and growing one. Apart from hot-water distribution—and even here certain grades of plastic perform quite satisfactorily, with nylon tube now being used on some central-heating systems—plastics are able to perform the job of other plumbing materials.

A short glossary of some of the main types may help to establish the role of plastics in plumbing

PVC is an abbreviation for polyvinyl chloride. The most widely used plastic, capable of handling moderately hot water, is unplasticized PVC, u/PVC. Another variant, similar in suitability, is c/PVC, or chlorinated PVC.

Polythene, in high-density and low-density forms (abbreviated to LD and HD) is widely used for storage cisterns. In pipework, the rigid HD polythene is used for sizes above 53 mm bore. A proprietary name used for polythene by ICI is Alkathene.

Perspex—an ICI trade name—made from methyl-methacrylate is the best known of this plastics family.

Polypropylene is another plastic suitable for use at a higher water temperature.

GRP, or glass-reinforced plastic, uses glass-fibre mat, bonded by polyester or epoxide resin.

ABS is another plastic, widely used for waste and soil systems. The abbreviation stands for acronitrile butadiene styrene.

Plastic traps and fittings, push-together pipe with 'o'-ring seals and solvent-weld jointing simplify the job of fitting and connecting up.

Thermal expansion must be allowed for, by type of fittings

26

or in the manner of connection. In some cases, in accordance with the manufacturer's instructions, expansion sections may have to be incorporated into the run of the pipe.

SOLVENT WELDING

Pipe is easily cut, using a fine-toothed hacksaw. First, cut the pipe square, and file off any internal burrs. Degrease the joint surfaces of both pipe and fitting, with cleaning fluid and an absorbent grease-free paper.

Slightly chamfer the outer edge of the pipe with a file at an angle of about 15°. Next, roughen the joint surfaces, using clean emery cloth, fine glasspaper or fine wire wool, and clean with fluid again.

Using a clean, small brush, apply an even layer of cement to both fitting and pipe in a lengthwise direction, with a thicker coating on the pipe. Make sure that no cleaning fluid remains as this would impair the effectiveness of the solvent. Also ensure that the mating surfaces are absolutely dry. The tin of cement must be closed immediately after use, as the solvent evaporates quickly. It is also highly inflammable, so smoking or naked flame must be avoided

Immediately push the fitting on to the pipe without turning it. Hold it for a few seconds and then wipe off surplus cement with a clean piece of cloth. Leave the joint undisturbed for at least five minutes and then handle only with reasonable care.

SCREWED PLASTIC JOINTS

With this type of joint, threads are cut with special tools and joints are tightened with strap-type tools. These rather special tools are best hired. Ptfe tape is wrapped in an anti-clockwise direction for $1\frac{1}{2}$ turns around the thread to make the thread watertight. Fittings are made in 6 mm ($\frac{1}{4}$ in) up to 51 mm (2 in). These pipes are thicker walled and more costly than the solvent-welded pipe. Screwed joints are not advisable in situations where there is excessive vibration.

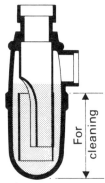

Fig. 1.
Maximum water seal

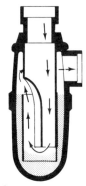

Fig. 2.
Action of trap under severe siphonage. Air is drawn through the central by-pass tube, but leaves sufficient water to re-seal the trap

Fig. 3.
End of siphonic action, with the trap providing a permanent seal

Design principle of the bottle trap

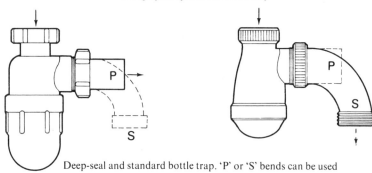

Deep-seal and standard bottle trap. 'P' or 'S' bends can be used

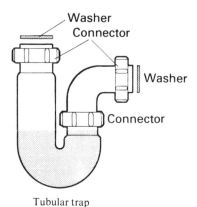

Washer
Connector
Washer
Connector

Tubular trap

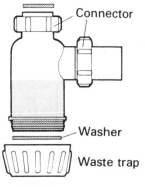

Connector
Washer
Waste trap

Bottle trap

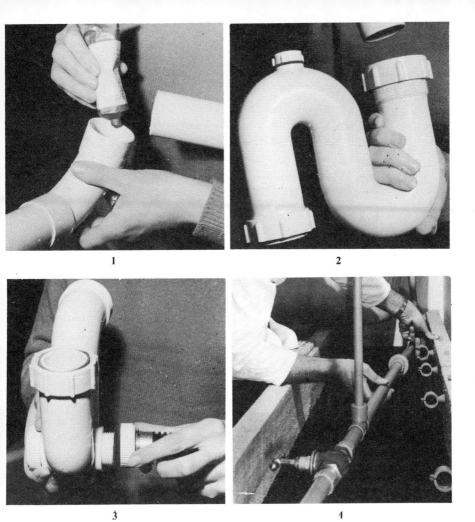

1. Applying solvent to mouth of plastic waste pipe to make welded joint

2. 'S' bath trap, showing inspection cap

3. 'P' trap, showing entry of overflow. This can be connected to either side of the trap (Ruberoid Ltd)

4. Complete cold-water supply system in plastic, with solvent-weld connections (Durapipe and Fittings Ltd)

PLASTIC COLD-WATER SERVICES

Up to a two-thirds saving in cost, compared with other materials, and a saving of 25% in installation time has been claimed for cold-water services made entirely in plastic. This is the experience of one manufacturer, Durapipe and Fittings Ltd, of West Drayton, Middlesex.

Up to about 30 m of pipe is needed to provide cold services for an average house. These services can be used fully with other plastic materials, such as plastic cold-water cisterns. Tee-pieces, elbows and sockets used with plastic-welding techniques, and plastic 'tap' connectors and cistern connectors dispense with expensive copper-to-plastic connectors. Screwed connections using 'O' ring seals should be hand tightened and then a further quarter of a turn with a spanner.

MECHANICAL JOINTS

Mechanical joints fall into two categories: compression fittings in which a rubber ring is compressed round the pipe by tightening a nut, for pipes of up to 54 mm (about 2 in); and push-fit rubber-ring ('o') joints to connect U/PVC pipe above 54 mm.

Mechanical joints are described as 'non-end-load taking', which means that pipe must be anchored securely in place so that the joint does not blow apart under pressure.

Mechanical joints provide an effective way of making repairs if the pipe becomes ruptured; the damaged portion is simply cut out and replaced by a fitting. This is done using a seal ring, which is placed over the spigot of the cast-iron pipe or fitting. The fitting is then gently heated with a blow torch, using a 'cool' flame, until the PVC shrinks over the ring and spigot to effect a seal.

Push-fit assembly of PVC pipe can be similarly made to cast-iron, salt-glazed or pitch-fibre pipe, using similar jointing techniques but incorporating ring-seals, to allow for thermal expansion.

If needed, a hot-lead joint can be made to cast-iron pipe in a system incorporating a ring seal, by using a special caulking bush.

ABS and PVC pipes can be bent by the application of heat. It is not possible to bend pipe over 28 mm diameter satisfactorily other than in a factory. Use a blow torch or hot-air gun. The heat should be applied gently along the run of the pipe, which is rotated continually, to ensure even softening. When the pipe becomes flexible, it should be bent slightly over the desired angle. Not all manufacturers advise this method of bending, recommending instead the use of elbows and bends.

The use of sleeving where PVC pipe passes through a wall is necessary to allow for thermal expansion. There must be a minimum air space of 75 mm (3 in) between PVC and any high-temperature heating mains. While PVC is a good thermal insulator, and water in these pipes will not freeze as readily as in metal pipes, it is desirable, for example in roof spaces, to lag PVC piping.

4

THE LAYOUT OF DOMESTIC PLUMBING

Modern plumbing services rely partially on a storage system for cold water, usually located in the loft. The main reason for a storage supply is to equalize the demand on the mains supply at any one time. Older types of system piped water direct to each tap and outlet and this could cause a heavy drain on the supply service if all taps were in use at one time. Also the mains supply is at a very high pressure, which causes more wear on pipe bores and fittings. High-pressure supply is obviously more noisy when filling and there is much greater likelihood of 'water hammer'—a vibratory condition of the pipes.

The older, direct-to-taps method is known as the 'direct system' and is not now permitted in new building. The modern storage method is called the 'indirect system'. Among the advantages are that if there is a break in the water supply for any reason, there is still a reservoir of water in the house. Also, there is less likelihood of an insanitary situation where, for example, it is not possible to flush a WC.

The domestic system begins and ends where the Water Board's supply terminates and the local authority's sewage-disposal arrangements provide connection to the main sewer. The Water Board's service can be cut off by means of the company's stopcock, usually located in the path just outside the house, which can be operated with a long key. It is a good idea to have a key to control this in case of need; it is possible to make a key from a long, stout piece of timber, with a wedge cut out of the centre at one end to fit onto the top of the stopcock. Some company stopcocks have a square head for which a special key is needed.

Usually, the mains supply to the consumer is by means of an underground lead pipe. This is laid by the water company and is terminated at the company's stopcock. It is then the

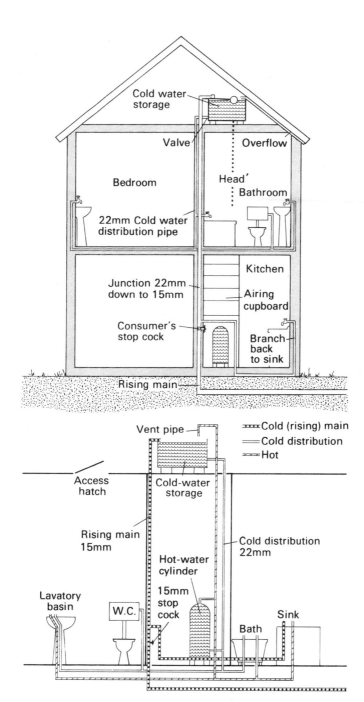

Two typical domestic plumbing layouts

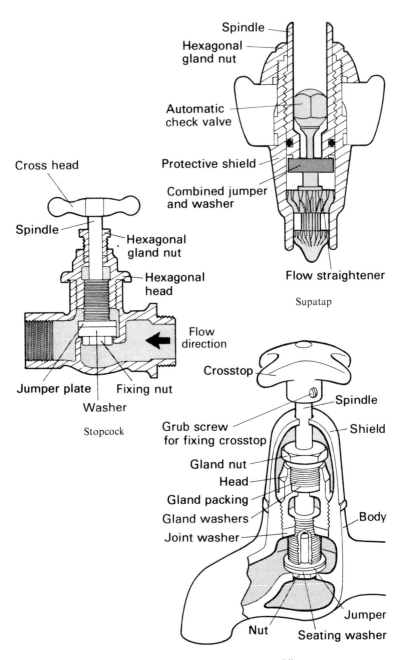

Spindle

Hexagonal gland nut

Automatic check valve

Protective shield

Combined jumper and washer

Flow straightener

Supatap

Cross head

Spindle

Hexagonal gland nut

Hexagonal head

Flow direction

Jumper plate   Fixing nut

Washer

Stopcock

Crosstop

Spindle

Shield

Grub screw for fixing crosstop

Gland nut

Head

Gland packing

Gland washers

Joint washer

Body

Jumper

Nut   Seating washer

Bib tap

consumer's responsibility to take the water on to his premises. Some water boards frown at a consumer's service which is continued other than in lead pipework, but many will now allow copper or heavy-duty polypropylene pipe to be used to take the domestic supply into the house. This supply is called the 'rising main' once it enters the home.

This pipe should be buried deep enough to avoid damage from implements used in the garden and below the 'frost line' (about 460 mm or 18 in). Most rising-main services are in pipes of 15 mm ($\frac{1}{2}$ in) bore. It is a good idea to provide your own stopcock just inside the premises as the company's stopcock can easily get covered over by activities such as the resurfacing of paths.

Among the most important requirements in a domestic plumbing system are the provision of safety devices such as ball valves, to terminate supply when cisterns are full, and the provision of overflows on storage cisterns and toilets.

Additional shut-off valves should be incorporated to isolate the outlets from the cistern into the hot-water cylinder. Overflows to the storage cistern and toilet cisterns can be made in polypropylene push-together plastic, or similar material, and routed so that any overflowing gives a prominent warning and can be quickly corrected. The pipe for this should be taken well clear of the house structure, and has to exceed the diameter of the flow service by being one size larger.

The system should also be capable of being shut down just inside the premises by a consumer's stopcock. This is a non-return valve, fitted into the supply system and located at some suitable and easy-to-reach spot. A common position is beneath the kitchen sink, for this is normally the point where the direct cold-water service is first taken, in order to provide a fresh-water supply at the kitchen tap. Another good position is in an airing or other cupboard, but care must be taken in the routing of pipework so that no involved or tortuous runs occur, since this may produce installation difficulties and could lead to air locks.

The stopcock body is marked with an arrow to indicate the direction of flow, since it allows water to flow only in one direction. This is in order to prevent the back flowing of water which could lead to the danger of pollution of the mains. Unless the stopcock is mounted the correct way round, it follows that no water can enter the system!

The supply pipe, after serving the sink, should be taken by the most direct route to feed the storage cistern. Here the ball valve, which can be adjusted to some extent, sets the level of the water and controls the supply. The storage cistern feeds the bath and wash-basin taps, WC's and cold supply to the hot-water heating system. This supply is by means of one or two outlets located at the bottom of the storage cistern.

STORAGE CISTERNS

Until recent years, these were usually made of galvanized steel and likely to corrode in time. The modern approach is to replace these with PVC or glass-fibre cisterns, the latter called GRP (glass-reinforced plastic). Some PVC cisterns can be folded and trussed with rope and jockeyed through a fairly small loft opening. These have the virtue of being very light to handle. Another material in which cisterns are made is asbestos.

The best location for the cold-water storage cistern is usually the loft, since apart from preventing annoyance caused by the noise of filling, it provides a high point to create a 'static head' or pressure of water at outlets.

This cistern is usually between 227 litres (50 gallons) and 363 litres (80 gallons) in capacity, dependent on the demands of the household. An average three-bredoomed household of four persons requires a minimum 227-litre capacity.

Disposal of an old cistern can sometimes be a problem, since this may have been fitted before the roof was completed—or tiles or slates may have been removed to facilitate its entry. One solution is to leave it in the loft after it has been unplumbed, since there is often abundant space in many lofts. If you want to remove it, you may need to cut it up with a metal saw.

However, that old, worn-out cistern may well be served by equally ancient pipe services, and the opportunity may be taken to replumb—and also to reposition the new cistern if there is any improvement of layout to be gained. Clearly, if the existing pipework requires no attention and the routing is satisfactory the terminations on your new cistern should be made to meet it—there is no virtue in making extra work!

A storage cistern is often incorrectly called a 'tank'—a term which is only correct when the storage cistern is sealed from atmospheric pressure, as older 'tank' storage arrangements were.

The cistern is served by a variety of pipe connections. It is supplied from the rising main by a 15 mm or $\frac{1}{2}$ in bore pipe. The supply is controlled by a ball valve, which shuts off the supply by means of an arm operated by a plastic or copper ball 'float'. As the name 'float' suggests, this lies on the surface of the cistern water. The float contains air and is buoyant and rises as the water flows in to switch off the inlet valve at a determined level. It is usually possible to adjust the cut-off level of the water, either by slightly bending the ball arm or by means of adjusting screws.

The supply from the mains is at a high pressure so it is essential to use the high-pressure type of valve. Do not confuse this with the low pressure type found in toilet cisterns, which are fed from the low-pressure side of the system—the storage cistern. As a refinement, a gate valve or a stopcock may be fitted into the rising main to shut down the supply to the cistern, allowing the main fresh-water supply to be maintained at the kitchen sink if you need at any time to shut off the internal supply.

As already stated, one or two feed pipes may be taken from the cistern, depending on the household demand. One may serve the hot-water circuit while the other supplies the domestic cold-water system. The supply to both should be adequate with a pipe of 15 mm ($\frac{1}{2}$ in) or 22 mm ($\frac{3}{4}$ in). If the demand for hot water is great, a 28 mm or 1 in supply can be provided to feed the hot-water cylinder.

The other pipework required is the overflow—one size larger than the incoming supply—and the expansion pipe taken from the crown of the hot-water cylinder. This is taken up over the cistern and curved over just above it to provide a

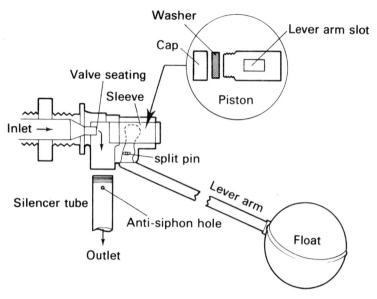

Detail of ball valve assembly

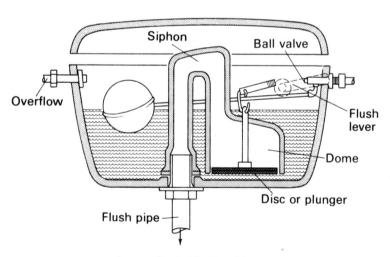

Layout of typical flushing cistern

hot-water expansion vent. This pipe should never be allowed to dip into the cistern, or circulation will be set up by siphonage, pumping hot water around the storage system!

INSTALLING A NEW CISTERN

To remove the old cistern first empty it. Shut down supply to the cistern and switch off all heating appliances served from the plumbing system, otherwise damage may be caused. Taps and any drain cocks should be opened to drain off the majority of the water. Since outflow connections are usually positioned at about 50 mm or 2 in. above the bottom of the cistern—to be above any 'sludge line'—the residue of water will need to be baled out. Connections are usually easily removed with adjustable spanners and any usable fittings can be kept.

The ball-valve assembly, for example, should be re-usable in the new cistern. A punctured ball can be unscrewed and replaced. The assembly should be inspected and any repairs or maintenance carried out. Details of how to do this appear in the chapter on maintenance.

It is a good idea to preplumb the new cistern as far as possible before lifting it into the loft. Hoes for the various pipe circuits can be cut. The opening for the ball valve should be about 75 mm (3 in) below the top of the cistern and be slightly larger than the threaded valve stem. Use a centre punch to mark the hole centre and a hole cutter or a large auger bit to make the hole, centred on the punch mark, as this prevents the cutter or auger from slipping.

There are two types of hole cutter—one with a number of interchangeable blades of various sizes and the other with an adjustable cutter on a bar. Both have a twist-drill centre, to make the pilot hole and provide a pivot. A hand drill is better than a power drill here, since plastic will heat up and be difficult to cut if drilling is carried out at speed. Use a file to remove any burrs left by drilling.

Ball-valve units may have two loose nuts on the stem. These go on either side of the wall of the cistern and allow adjustments to be made for the amount of projection of the

39

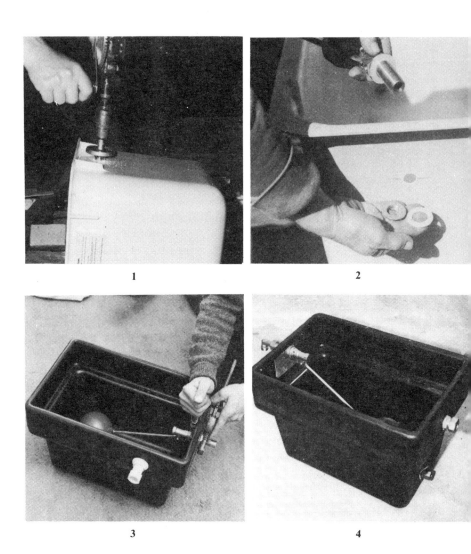

COLD-WATER CISTERNS

1. Hole cutter used to drill aperture in glass-fibre cistern, to accept fittings

2. Polypropylene washers are fitted on either side of stem of ball valve. Note the lock nut

3. Two spanners used to lock ball-valve assembly in place on a plastic cistern

4. Assembled cistern, showing overflow and cold-feed connections

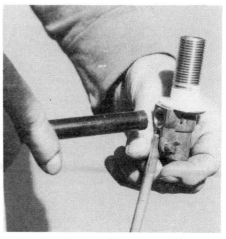

5 6

7

5. Ball-valve assembly in place in a storage cistern

6. How the silencer pipe attaches to a storage cistern's ball valve.

7. Hot-water expansion pipe taken over the top of the storage cistern

stem. Another type has a single nut, positioned on the outside cistern wall. Plastic or fibre washers are placed on either side of the wall before the nuts are locked tight.

To the stem of the valve assembly one should attach a swivel compression 'tap' connector, which contains a loose fibre washer, forming a water-tight joint when the nut of the connection is tightened.

The incoming rising main feeds in to the other end of the connector. The ball assembly can then be screwed to the threaded end of the arm and an anti-noise pipe screwed into the stem of the valve. This pipe projects into the water, so that the incoming supply is introduced below the water level.

Terminations to and from the cistern can be straight or angled—to suit the position of your pipe runs.

The cistern should be stood on sturdy pieces of timber such as 100 mm × 50 mm (4 in × 2 in), set end up across the joists. Two or three pieces should be used to spread the weight of a cistern. GRP cisterns should be supported over the entire bearing area.

Overflow fittings can be in plastic, as can the overflow pipe. These can be of the 'push-fit' variety where the pipe simply pushes together. The over-flow pipe should come out clear of obstruction to allow a continuous fall and be in a position where it is immediately observed if in operation, otherwise much water may be wasted.

Where capillary fittings are used for connection near a plastic or GRP cistern, take care to protect the sides from heat.

Once connections are made, the cistern can be filled. Check carefully for leaks and drain down if there are any 'weeping' connections. Avoid trying to tighten these with water in the cistern—there is a danger that you could release a flood!

The ball valve is adjusted finally when the cistern is almost full and is set so that the water level is at least 25 mm or 1 in below the overflow pipe. To do this you will have to bend the ball arm very carefully or turn the adjustment screw provided on some valves.

To test the function, draw off a small quantity of water and observe the refilling and cut off. After about a day, check that the functions are all satisfactory, that there are no seepages, and that the ball-valve is working accurately. It is a good idea to make a lid on the cistern if one is not supplied. One can be made from blockboard, chipboard or building boards of various types. This will keep the cistern free of the dust which seeps through unlined roofs, as are generally found in older houses. A hole should be made in the lid to admit the hot-water vent pipe.

Any loft insulation should be removed from beneath the cistern so that heat from the house can perrcolate through and help to prevent freezing in cold weather. Cisterns should always be lagged against freezing conditions.

DOMESTIC HOT WATER

Hot-water services in older installations frequently consist of a square galvanized storage tank, heated by a kitchen solid-fuel boiler or, possibly, by an immersion heater. The latter tend to be located in airing cupboards.

The modern approach uses a hot-water cylinder, which is not only stronger than the old-fashioned galvanized tank but will not rust or corrode. The standard hot-water cylinder is 915 mm (36 in) high × 460 mm (18 in) in diameter. The bottom is concave or 'dished' to provide strength, while the top is domed or 'crowned' to prevent air locks from occurring.

There are two basic types of cylinder—the direct and the indirect. In the former, the water being heated is that which is drawn off. The indirect cylinder contains an inner jacket, or calorifier, which heats the surrounding, draw-off water; the two waters do not commingle.

A variation is the self-priming cylinder. Here the two waters are separated by an air bubble. The water in the cylinder should not be allowed to reach boiling point, or the bubble will disperse, the waters will mingle, and you will have to allow the water to cool so that the bubble can re-form.

Frequently, the hot-water cylinder is part of a central-heating system. Here the water may be heated by what is called natural circulation or gravity flow. This works on the

43

principle that the molecules of hot water expand, and as they do so, a circulation of water is set up. The molecules of the cooling water contract and thus return to the heating source, where the water is reheated and recycles through the pipes and cylinder.

For this principle a minimum bore of 22 mm to 28 mm is necessary for the 'primary' flow-and-return pipework. A more modern principle operates on what is called the 'pumped system' primary. This is part of a sophisticated central-heating system and a special type of indirect cylinder, known as a high-recovery Grade 1 cylinder, is desirable but not essential. Where a conventional cylinder, with older, conventional heating systems, will heat and recycle from cold in about an hour, the high-recovery unit takes about half this time. However, the self-priming cylinder cannot be used in this connection, for the pump action would liberate the air bubble.

In either case the fresh water of the hot water supply and the 'dead' circulating water of the central heating system are kept separate. Fresh water is 'live', containing a high quantity of oxygen in the form of air bubbles. When a central heating system is put into operation, these bubbles boil out to a high point in the circuit, usually a radiator, when the air can be released by opening an air valve. This is called 'purging' or 'bleeding' the circuits. Where live water can lead to air locking and corrosion, 'dead' circulating water, contained in the circuit, will not corrode or cause scaling in pipework.

A direct cylinder can be adapted to serve as an indirect one by means of a hot-water circulating coil, resembling an immersion-heater coil. This has advantages where an existing direct cylinder needs conversion to indirect use when a heating system is installed or modernized. This type of element is used on the pumped-primary heating circuit.

Immersion heaters are usually 1 kW or 2 kW in rating and preferably should be on their own separate circuit. They are thermostatically regulated, allowing temperature settings between 48·9°C (120°F) and 82·2°C (180°F). A satisfactory setting for domestic needs is 60°C (140°F). Metric 4 m² cable should be used for connecting.

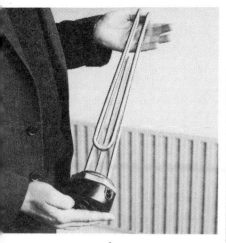

1

2

3

HOT-WATER CYLINDERS

1. Standard electric immersion heater element. This screws into a boss at the top of the hot-water cylinder

2. Fibre washer provides seal at boss for immersion heater

3. Lagging a hot-water cylinder is important. Picture shows a proprietary lagging jacket

There are two basic types of heater—the dual and the single-stage coil. As hot water stratifies and rises, the water at the crown of the cylinder will be rather hotter than that lower down the cylinder. The two-stage heater allows the water to be heated selectively. It consists of two elements—one longer than the other—enabling merely the crown of the cylinder to be heated for light use such as washing or washing up, and the longer element to heat the full contents of the cylinder for baths. Water stratifies when heated to such an extent that there can be an appreciable difference in temperature in a cylinder in the space of a few millimetres.

Immersion heaters screw into a screwed boss opening, usually in the crown of the cylinder, and one should be chosen that is for the correct length in relation to the height of the cylinder. A ring of hemp and non-toxic plumbing compound can be used to form a washer, or a purpose-made rubber ring, with a smear of compound on each face, to consolidate the joint, can be used to effect a seal. The heater tightens into the boss opening, from which the sealing plate is first unscrewed and removed. The unit should be tightened home against its sealing washers with a large Stillson-pattern wrench. Great care should be taken to avoid excess tightening or the cylinder may be ruptured. Though structurally strong overall, a cylinder is vulnerable at its points of connection.

Other connections on the cylinder—of the threaded, male-iron type—provide hot-water draw-off, from the cylinder crown, and cold feed, from the cold-water storage cistern, to a point about a quarter of the way up the cylinder. The primary connections are located on the opposite side, again about a quarter of the way up, and a similar distance down from the top. The hot-water primary connection is the higher of the two. If a boiler is being used, the primary connections are made to the top and bottom terminations in the same way.

The vent-pipe, taken from the crown of the cylinder and curved over above the loft cold-water cistern, is a safety precaution, for though hot water will expand up the vent pipe for perhaps 1—$1\frac{1}{2}$ m, it will seldom vent into the cistern, unless very high temperatures are attained in heating the cylinder.

Sometimes taps are some distance from the cylinder and a large amount of cold water would have to be drawn off and wasted. To avoid this, a system of secondary circulation can be installed. This is achieved by the normal draw-off connection, with a return circuit located above this point and returning, ultimately, below it. When water is drawn from the hot tap, the secondary circulation is broken (see diagram).

Once charged with water, the cylinder can be substantially heavy. It should be positioned on stout pieces of timber, set across the direction of joists and with space beneath, the latter to allow air circulation which will prevent condensation.

A gate valve should be incorporated in the cold-water feed near the cylinder and a drain cock should also be fitted to enable the cylinder to be drained down.

The hot-water cylinder is frequently and usually best located in the airing cupboard, where the dissipation of heat is put to good use. However, excessive venting of heat is costly, and the cylinder should be insulated with one of the proprietary foam, glass-fibre or mineral wool jackets.

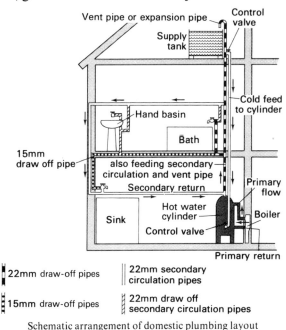

Schematic arrangement of domestic plumbing layout

47

KITCHEN PLUMBING

Plumbing in the kitchen may be part of a major kitchen replan. If for example, doors or windows are repositioned to make better use of space, it will usually follow that the plumbing will also have to be turned round. In redesigning a kitchen it is a good idea to consider fitting labour-saving appliances such as waste-disposal units, a hygienic development which some authorities have frowned on until quite recently, and consider fitting a dishwasher, which is a useful place to store dishes after they are washed until the next meal. A washing machine is a 'must' for many homes, and these can be operated with temporary plumbing if desired, by means of flexible hoses. It is a better idea to plumb the washing machine in permanently if there is space and facility to do so.

A new sink unit may not always match up to existing plumbing, particularly if an existing set of taps were of the 'bib' or wall-mounted variety. The modern sink unit is usually fitted with fixing holes to admit pillar taps.

The plan of campaign here must be the same as for plumbing elsewhere—preplan and have everything to hand, and avoid depriving the household for water for any lengthy period of time.

KITCHEN SINKS

Stainless-steel, vitreous-enamelled steel and plastic types of surface, including plasticized stainless steel, offer a wide selection of easy-to-fit sinks. Single and double drainers, left- and right-handed units and single and double bowls add up to a versatile choice of layouts. The old 'butler's sink', made of fireclay, is not designed to fit modern kitchen units and has become largely outdated. The fitting of a new sink will often displace one of these older types.

Waste outlets on modern sinks are normally of $1\frac{1}{4}$ in or 35 mm diameter. If a waste disposal unit is fitted, as described later in this chapter, the outlet will need to be larger or capable of enlargement.

The modern sink top is supported by its base cabinet. Brackets and fixing rails, the latter fitted into the flanged end of the sink top, are the usual ways of fixing this to the base unit. The methods may vary in detail, according to the sink top and base unit used, and the appropriate maker's instructions should be followed.

Taps, which may be single or mixer types, are based in a thin rim of non-hardening mastic or use polypropylene washers. A plastic 'top hat' connector screws on to the tails of the taps from beneath and lock-nuts are tightened on the tails. 'Tap' and swivel connectors, straight or angled, are tightened on to the tails for connection to the hot and cold supply.

Connecting principles are broadly the same for fixing mixers as for individual taps, with hot and cold connections made to the appropriate stems. The mixing function is within the actual body of the unit.

The cold connection is usually a 15 mm ($\frac{1}{2}$ in) supply from the rising main, the service being continued in 15 mm pipe to feed the cold storage supply. The simplest and usually the best way of serving the kitchen tap is by a tee-piece branch connection.

Once the sink top is firmly positioned, check that the pipes meet the supply pipes. The angles of the taps can be checked, adjusted and finally tightened. The waste is then fitted. A rubber washer goes into the outlet and the waste grill is then fixed by means of a centre bolt. A washer is fitted over the waste connector which is screwed on to the threaded sink outlet.

Check that the trap outlet is in line with the waste outlet before screwing the trap on to the outlet stem. Traps can be of the tubular or of the bottle variety. Lead and copper may be fitted where existing services are being replumbed. However, plastic outlet arrangements are usually quicker and simpler to fit for initial installation or for replacement.

A variety of traps and connections are adjustable, which

enables the connection to be made easily. Overflows usually screw into place and may be connected by a flexible tube to the side of the waste outlet.

WASHING MACHINES

While automatic washing machines can be connected up for temporary use, it is generally a more convenient arrangement to plumb them in as permanent installations. This description of how to plumb in a washing machine applies to a Hoover Automatic de Luxe, made by Hoover Ltd., of Perivale, Greenford, Middlesex. The techniques for plumbing in other makes of unit are, however, similar and this provides a general guide to the principles.

Some washing machines only require connection to the cold supply. Other machines, such as this, require both hot and cold supplies. Supply is in 15 mm or $\frac{1}{2}$ in pipe. Connections to the appliance are made with flexible pipes, connected to the back of the machine. These are longer than usually needed for permanent connection. Allow sufficient flexibility for the unit to be pulled out for access. These pipes are connected by hose clips and unions to hot and cold supply pipes.

As an alternative to connection to a hot tap or storage supply, hot water can be supplied by an independent source or a back boiler—gas or electric storage system—including immersion heaters, or multiple-outlet instantaneous gas heaters with external flue, provided these have sufficient hot-water pressure available. Single-outlet gas and electric heaters must never be used.

A 2.44 m (8 ft) water head is the minimum needed on both hot and cold supply, equal to 0·28 bar (4 lb/sq in) with a maximum of 10.5 bar (150 lb/sq in). Pipework connections

1. 'Drifting' lock nut on the base of a kitchen waste assembly

2. Connecting a pillar tap assembly to a sink unit

3. Making connection to the stem of a kitchen tap, using a compression-ended 'tap' connector

4. Fitting the 76 mm waste for a waste-disposal unit

5. Fixing body of waste-disposal unit to chassis housing on waste outlet

6. 'O'-ring seal fitted to the motor cartridge
/ . . .

1

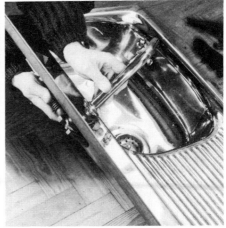

2

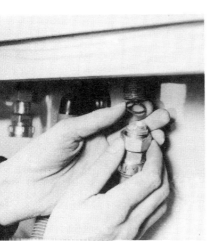

3

4

5

6

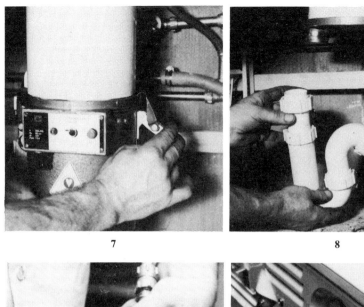

7   8

9   10

. . . /

7. Cartridge fixes to body by means of clips

8. Tubular trap, suitable for use with waste-disposal unit as well as for kitchen waste generally

9. Metal circlip used to connect flexible pipe to washing machine

10. Clip-on connectors on back of washing machine (Hoover Ltd)

should be provided with shut-down valves to facilitate removal of the machine. Usually, tee-pieces can be connected to provide a branch from the supply services.

All pipework should be clipped to the wall surface and brought in unobtrusively. Once pipe stems are prepared, the flexible hoses are pushed over the pipes and hose clips tightened on to this supply pipework. These can be given a smear of soap, so that the pipes can be pushed well home to ensure leak-proof operation.

To prevent water from siphoning from the machine, it is necessary to incorporate in the permanent waste pipe an air-break or a vent to the atmosphere. This should be at least 460 mm (18 in) above the level on which the machine stands.

Usually the best way to achieve this is to use a stand-pipe of 35 mm ($1\frac{1}{4}$ in) minimum diameter, into the top of which the crooked end of the drain hose of the machine can be fitted. Mount the stand-pipe so that the top is 790 mm (27 in) above the floor level. When the outlet hose is inserted into the stand-pipe the end of the outlet hose will be at the prescribed height.

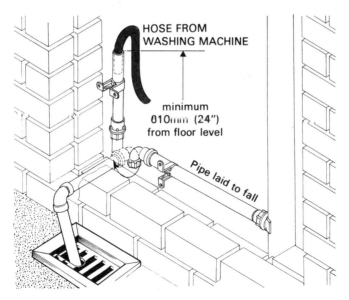

HOSE FROM
WASHING MACHINE

minimum
810mm (24")
from floor level

Pipe laid to fall

Typical washing-machine connections

53

The gap between the rubber crooked hose and the bore of the stand-pipe provides the necessary airbreak to avoid siphoning. The lower end of the stand-pipe can then be taken away to a drain, observing the general rule that a drain should have a gentle fall throughout its length.

The 35 mm plastic stand and drainage pipe should be clipped to the wall with plastic clips and a hole cut in the wall at the bottom. A plug-cutter attachment in a rotary unit is a satisfactory way of doing this.

On the outside wall slope the waste pipe gently to the drain, fixing this with clips to the wall. Plastic 25 mm pipe with push-on elbows is suitable. The pipe can be simply cut, using a fine-toothed hacksaw.

The machine must be connected to a 13-amp ring main or a separate point not below this rating, with a three-pin plug. Finally, open the shut-down valves to enable the machine to operate.

DISHWASHERS

Plumbing in a dishwasher is a similar operation to that with a washing machine. It can also be operated as a permanently plumbed in unit or temporarily connected. The unit described here is the Kenwood dishwasher, made by Tricity Ltd., of Havant, Hants.

As a dishwasher is in daily use, the most convenient position in the kitchen should be chosen. It can be installed as a permmanent feature under a working top, between kitchen units, on a working top, or mounted at a convenient height on the wall. Here we describe the fitting of a unit beneath a sink top. It can be mounted on a plinth to bring it up to fit snugly beneath a double drainer. The basic connections are a 15 mm ($\frac{1}{2}$ in) hot-water supply and a 22 mm ($\frac{3}{4}$ in) drainage outlet.

In most cases, the water demands in the kitchen do not preclude feeding the dishwasher from the hot tap supply, and a 15 mm compression equal tee can be simply fitted into the circuit to supply the appliance, with an additional stopcock at the terminal end. A connection can then be made using a hose

54

ferrule fitted on to the stopcock.

With the supply from the storage cistern, a satisfactory connection can be made by fitting a short piece of extension tube to the stopcock, to enable the flexible feed hose to be fed on and fixed with a hose clip.

Service to the machine can enter from the left or the right. A minimum clearance of 25 mm (1 in) behind the machine allows the service to enter at any height. The 22 mm ($\frac{3}{4}$ in) outlet pipe slides inside the drain house and fixes with a hose clip. A bending spring can be used to incorporate a dip in the pipework, to provide a water-seal trap.

It is important that the drain pipe connector is in the highest part of the drain line—a maximum height of 1 m (about 3 ft).

The 22 mm pipe, which can be plastic, copper or stainless steel, is taken out through a wall. This pipe should be clipped to the outside wall and drained into the sink waste outlet, maintaining a gentle fall. The pipe is best introduced below a sink grating or through a back inlet gulley.

The drain hose is in two pieces and its direction of exit can be arranged by slackening one of the clips and afterwards re-tightening these. The machine should be provided with a separate power point or connected to a standard 13-amp ring main, using a three-pin connection.

WASTE-DISPOSAL UNITS

Waste-disposal units are becoming increasingly popular; these can be fitted quickly and with little modification to the existing plumbing at the kitchen sink. The unit located beneath the sink provides for efficient and hygienic disposal of nearly all kitchen wastes, with only one or two exceptions —notably plastics, aluminium milk-bottle tops and, in some cases, banana skins, which are fibrous and tend to wrap round the mechanism of the unit. Units operate by means of an electric motor driving impeller and shredder blades which reduce the waste to a paste, disposed of through the normal sink drainage.

Disposers need an ordinary 13 amp electricity supply but it

is advisable, for reasons of safety, either to provide a pull switch or to locate any wall switch well away from the sink, siting it so that no hazard is caused by the proximity of water and the attendant possibility of electric shocks from wet hands!

There are various proprietary makes, all following a similar principal of fitting and operation. As the sink waste outlet may have to be enlarged, it is possible to specify, for a number of makes of unit, a hole of the required diameter. The standard sink outlet is 38 mm ($1\frac{1}{2}$ in) The waste-disposal unit requires an opening of 89 mm ($3\frac{1}{2}$ in). In some cases, notably with cast-iron sinks, a new sink will be needed, since the outlet cannot be satisfactorily enlarged. This may also be the case with enamelled surfaces, which may chip, and become unhygienic and prove to rust, as a result of cutting an enlarged hole. Hole-cutting saws, and where necessary recessing equipment, can be hired from manufacturers of a number of makes of unit.

The order of installation is first to disconnect the existing sink outlet and waste trap. The hole can be cut by a simple saw, resembling a junior hacksaw. In fact, it is practicable, on some grades of steel, to use this. A circular hole cutter can also be employed to enlarge the hole. Any rough edges can be smoothed with a rounded file.

The technique described here is for the unit made by Econa Parkamatic of Shirley, Solihull, Warwicks. The principles are much the same with other makes of unit, and all provide detailed installation instructions. First, the sink bush is coated on the underside of the lip with mastic sealant and then fitted over the sink waste opening. Next, the clamp seal, clamp plate and keyhole plate can be fitted over the lower flange of the sink bush. A circlip is then fitted in the lower recesses of the sink bush and should be partially tightened by three grub screws.

The waste-outlet assembly can then be fitted to the top housing. After this the outlet seal can be fitted over the end of the outlet bend, with the lip of the seal protruding through the outlet plate. The seal and the outer bend locate in the aperture in the top housing. Both outlet plate screws locate through the plate and are uniformly tightened.

Next, the top housing is fitted. The flat seal is positioned on the top of this housing. Heads of the fixing screws insert into the keyhole plate holes on the housing and turn clockwise until the top fixing screws butt against the ends of the slots. After this, turn the whole unit clockwise until the outlet bend matches the position of the waste pipe. The top housing can then be temporarily removed and the grub screws uniformly tightened. Then the top housing is refitted and turned till the top fixing screws butt against the slot ends. These screws are then uniformly tightened.

After this the outlet bend can be fitted to the waste-pipe trap. This should have a minimum fall of $7\frac{1}{2}°$ but a fall of 15° is better. A tubular trap should be substituted for a trap of bottle pattern, since the shallower tubular trap will be less prone to sedimentation.

On a number of models a reversing switch is incorporated on the body of the unit; this allows the mechanism to be freed in case of jamming. An advantage with some models, including the Econa Parkamatic range, is the provision of a dummy plate. This can be fitted in place of the motor body if a fault requires its removal and servicing, enabling the sink to continue in use. The body of the unit removes by unstrapping spring clips.

Where plastic outlet pipes are used, the body of the unit should be earthed separately.

A final stage is to check for smooth and leak-free running. Leaks are unlikely, but if they do occur, they can usually be cured by checking and resetting seals and general assembly.

It is important to ensure that the sink, as such, is firmly fixed at all points, as vibration may otherwise be set up and fixings on the waste-disposal unit can work loose.

The 38 mm ($1\frac{1}{2}$ in) waste pipe should be taken into a grilled gully to avoid leaving external deposits. Where discharge is into a septic tank, this should have a capacity of at least 5,000 litres (500 gallons).

BATHROOM PLUMBING

Bathrooms, particularly in older properties, frequently call for drastic updating. It is here that the festoons of thick, cumbrous pipe are most noticeable, often giving off a brown dispirited dribble of water at the taps.

Here, the plan of campaign must be at its most concerted. Very careful, detailed planning is necessary. Among the questions and problems which present themselves are how to make the best use of space and achieve the shortest run of pipework to services.

The first consideration, in any updating, is that of the equipment. Baths are still made in cast iron, which retains heat, but pressed-steel enamelled baths and plastic baths are becoming increasingly popular.

It is a good idea to consider incorporating a shower, either as a mixer attachment to the tap, or as a separately plumbed-in unit. You can, if space allows, opt for a separate shower cubicle. Water heaters, too, can be incorporated in bathrooms. In fact, you should give most careful thought not only as to how the space is to be reutilized but how modern equipment and appliances will fit into this scheme of things.

The usual vitreous china predominates in WC systems, basins and bidets—the latter a desirable addition if space allows you to incorporate one—but plastics are gradually gaining a foothold here as well.

Apart from baths, basins and toilets, shower cubicles and trays, taps are also made in hard, unbreakable plastic, as well as the usual chromed brassware. Plastic has the advantage of having a lower temperature to the touch compared with metal taps.

Sanitary ware is usually supplied with gummed paper edging to protect the units from transit damage and during fixing. Do not remove the paper until units are finally fixed or attempt to scrape it off, as this could damage surfaces. Always soak the paper off.

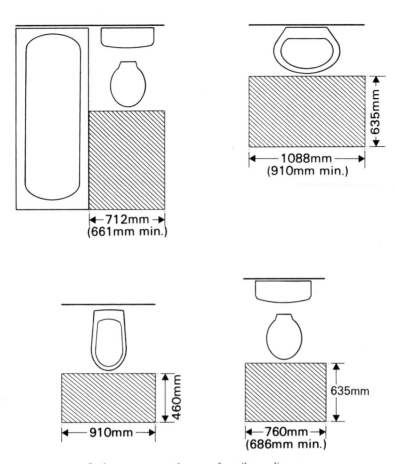

Optimum space requirements for toilet appliances

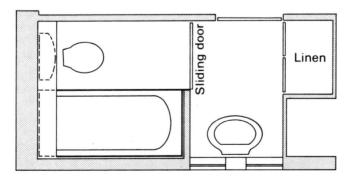

Space-saving layout for bathroom and toilet

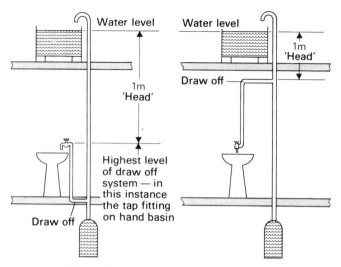

How the 'head' of Domestic water is determined

Before replacing any fitting or appliance, turn off the water. Any storage cisterns should be flushed to empty them. If stopcocks are fitted to the outlet side of the main cold cistern, it is obviously not necessary to drain down what is a large quantity of water.

Where sanitary ware is merely being updated, or replaced because of damage, it is a good idea to try to replace this with equipment of equivalent size and position of fittings, so that unnecessary re-routing of pipework is avoided.

WASH BASINS

Basins fall into three types—the pedestal, which rests on a vitreous-china centre column; the wall-hung basin, fixed to the wall by a mounting bracket; and the inset or built-in basin, used, for example, in vanitory units. Mounting fittings depend on the maker's design of unit.

To remove an old wash basin, after shutting off the water supply, unscrew the locking nut at the top of the waste trap, which allows this to fall clear of the basin. Next unscrew the connecting nuts under the taps. A basin wrench, which is angled to facilitate use in unscrewing basin fittings, will make this job easier. The old basin can then be unscrewed from the wall and the pedestal, if present, similarly unscrewed at the base.

In replacing or fitting sanitary ware, it is important to avoid the direct connection of metal to china. Washers, of plastic, leather, cork or rubber, should be used to avoid tension which may crack the basin.

Taps, wastes and overflows should be set in a thin rim of mastic, such as metal-glazing putty or proprietary plumbing putty, which never fully hardens and allows for expansion and contraction. Excess mastic will be pressed out by the action of tightening up the fitting and can then easily be trimmed off. Once taps are set in the basin, fit a washer and back nut on to the tap 'tails' and then tighten with a basin wrench or spanner.

On wastes, apply putty to the flange, insert the fitting into the outlet and fit rubber washers beneath, then fit and tighten the back locking nut.

With a bracket-mounted basin, first fix the bracket to the wall, lining this up carefully with a level and fixing firmly, using wall plugs as necessary. Locate the basin, so that the fitting projects through the centre hole of the bracket and fit a leather washer and a flanged back nut over the waste. Hand tighten the nut and then lock this firmly with a spanner. Location pins on the basin fit through the rear of the bracket. Fit rubber and metal washers on to these and, finally, tighten up the wing nuts. All these components should be part of the tap and the basin 'kit'.

Swivel tap connectors, 15 mm or $\frac{1}{2}$ in, are used to connect the water supply to basins. One end of the fitting is threaded and screwed on to the tap tails. Usually, a fibre washer completes the union. If the fitting is not of this type, wrap ptfe tape round the pipe for $1\frac{1}{2}$ turns in an anti-clockwise direction. The connection can then be tightened with a basin wrench or a spanner. Next, fit the trap to the waste fitting and tighten the locking nut. Water can then be turned on and the system can be checked for leaks. Any slight tendency to weep can usually be corrected by slight further tightening of connections.

On pedestal units the basin is screw fixed to the wall and the pedestal similarly fixed to the floor. Wing nuts again usually complete the union between basin and pedestal.

A crossover system of pipework can be mounted inside the pedestal, which is recessed at the back. This obviates a series of very acute bends, which should be avoided since they create turbulence and constrict water flow. The pedestal has the advantage of enabling this concealment of pipework. Pipe manipulation is carried out with taps, waste and related fittings in place but before the pedestal is finally screwed to the floor. This enables connections to be 'tried for size'. In any event, the space available for adjustment with the pedestal fixed would usually preclude adjustment and manipulation.

Bottle traps are preferred on wash basins as the deep seals are a help in preventing siphonage. These are simply tightened on to the waste outlet and connected to the domestic waste by means of lock nuts which tighten an 'o'-ring seal with plastic wastes, while wastes in lead and copper contain a washer to effect the seal. Remember to tighten these by hand and then apply a further quarter of a turn using grips.

Overflow outlets are usually built into the body of the basin and feed into the waste outlet once this is fitted.

BIDETS

The bidet is becoming increasingly popular, though in many bathrooms it may be difficult to fit for lack of space. A great effort is being made to popularize the bidet on the grounds of its health and sanitary advantages. This item is plumbed in in a similar manner to the wash basin and is similar in its

WASH BASINS

1. Basin waste bedded in plumber's mastic

2. Tightening the lock nut after fitting waste outlet

3. Fitting basin in housing on pedestal

4. Bottle-trap assembly fitted to the basin after this has been fixed to pedestal

5. 'Tap' connector, to connect supply to tap tails, contains a fibre sealing washer

6. Assembled basin pipework, showing neat 'slow-bend' pipework crossover behind pedestal

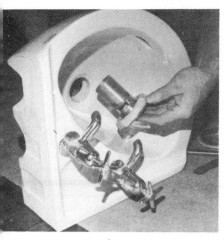

1

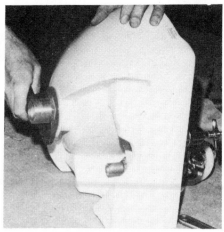

2

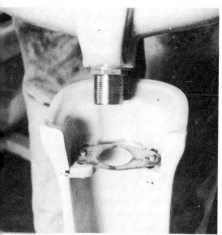

3

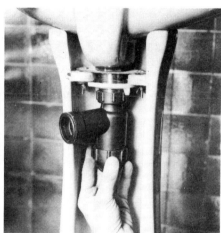

4

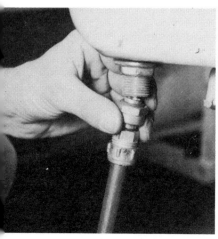

5

6

1   2

BIDETS

1. Connections for bidet are similar to those of wash basin

2. Bidets incorporate a flushing device but outlet arrangements are as for a standard wash basin

plumbing requirements. A hot and cold supply is fed to a mixer-tap unit and waste connections are made in 35 mm diameter pipe. In other respects, mounting this is as for a WC pan.

WC SYSTEMS

Domestic WC suites differ largely in the type of cistern. The main categories are the high-level, the mid-level and the low-

WCs

1. Pan connector is fitted to glazed soil pipe; note tarred rope gasket partly in place

2. Pan is slotted into connector and also sealed at this point with rope gasket, and finally collared with mortar

3. Plastic pan connector used to join outlet to plastic soil pipe

4. Connector can also be fitted to glazed soil pipe

5. Connecting pan to outlet with plastic connectors

6. Pan should be screwed to floor to prevent movement which may cause damage

/ . . .

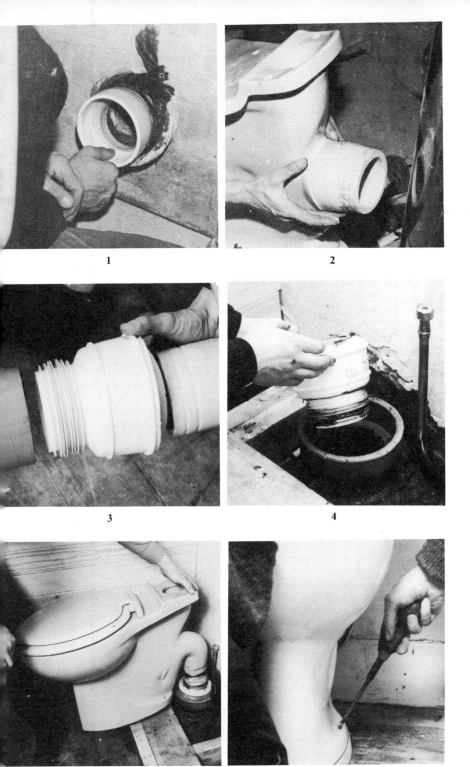

1

2

3

4

5

6

7

8

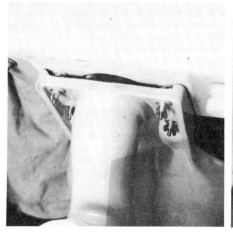

9

10

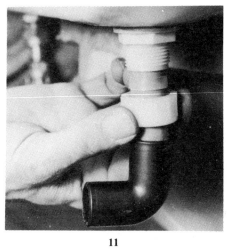

11

level cistern. Two types of low-flush suite are wash-down pan and the close-coupled suite. A further type of low-flush unit has a wall-attached WC pan and is known as a corbel closet. Most modern cisterns are made of plastic or vitreous china. The older types of cistern were usually of the high-level pattern, with a body of cast iron.

The average capacity of a cistern is about 10 litres (2 gallons) or 12 litres ($2\frac{1}{2}$ gallons). Cisterns are mostly reversible, allowing supply to be brought in on either side. In assembling the internal mechanism, account has to be taken of on which side supply is made.

Both high-and low-flush cisterns are joined to the WC pan in a similar way. A 38 mm plastic flush pipe is connected to the cistern by a nut and washer; one end of this pipe has a curved section which fits into the rear of the pan and is covered by a rubber cone, slotted over the stem at the point of pan entry. Flush pipe can be cut to length and is made so that sections can be slotted and joined together. When fitting a low-level cistern, adhere to the manufacturer's recommended length of flush pipe, or you may lack a sufficient head of water for efficient flushing. A high-level cistern of the older pattern can, normally be removed and replaced by a modern low-flush cistern, updating the look of the WC system.

A typical siphonic close-coupled suite is assembled by placing the cistern in position over the pan and joining it with two locking screws which tighten a rubber gasket around the joint to provide the water seal.

To assemble the ball valve and associated mechanism, first fit the siphon. This 'sits' in the cistern with the dome or piston housing on the same side as the ball valve, which is either 102 mm (4 in) or 114 mm ($4\frac{1}{2}$ in). The ball is on the opposite side to the dome. Take care that the siphon housing is centred when tightening the large nut which fixes it.

. . . /

7. Ring seal on outlet of one type of low-flush WC cistern

8. Connection on another pattern of low-flush cistern

9. Most low-flush cisterns lock in place by means of wing nuts on bolts

10. Supply connection to a WC cistern, using compression-ended coupling

11. Plastic overflow outlet with elbow fitting

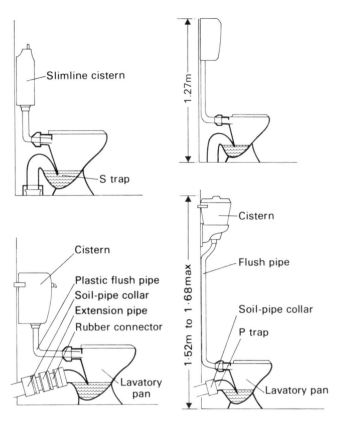

Connectors and extension pieces can be used to bring forward the WC position

When assembling the ball-valve, make sure that the float and arm have adequate clearance between cistern wall and siphon unit. This arm may need to be bent slightly to give clearance and to set the water level. Also make sure that the valve is of a low-pressure (storage supply) type. A silencer pipe should be fitted to cut down filling noise.

Straight or angled compression fittings are connected to the bulkhead fitting which houses the ball-valve assembly. These must be of the female-threaded 'tap' type. The fitting should again contain a fibre washer to provide an adequate water seal. The other end of the filling is connected to the supply from the storage cistern, made in 15 mm ($\frac{1}{2}$ in) tube.

Wall fixings for cisterns vary from screw holes in the top

68

part of the casing to vertical suspension brackets. It is important to ensure that firm fixings are made. Surfaces should be plugged and drilled for screw fixing. It is worth considering fixing a backing board and anchoring the cistern to this. Overflows, one size larger than supply, merely lock in place with a washer and nut, attached to a bulkhead fixing. Plastic elbows enable the overflow to be directed out behind the toilet.

WC pans terminate with a water-trap bend, called either a 'p' or an 's' bend. The former serves usually to provide an outlet connection through a wall; the latter is normally a

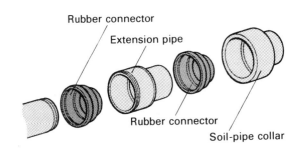

Rubber connector

Extension pipe

Rubber connector

Soil-pipe collar

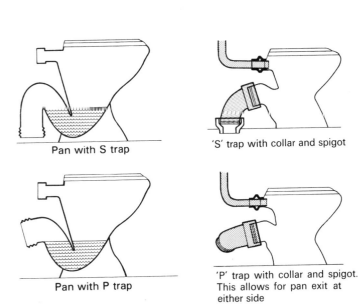

Pan with S trap

'S' trap with collar and spigot

Pan with P trap

'P' trap with collar and spigot. This allows for pan exit at either side

69

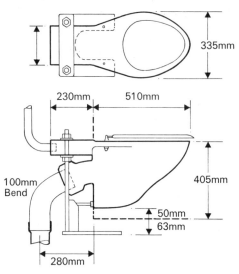

The corbel closet is cantilevered from the wall and not supported at the floor. Careful installation is, therefore, important

floor outlet. As Building Regulations now stipulate that new installations must have the soil stack pipe situated internally, the requirements for new installations frequently call for the 's' trap. Some models of pan are supplied with a choice of 'p' or 's' trap and also allow a simple outlet connection to be made on either side of the pan, without the addition of extra connecting pieces.

Since the principle of fitting a new pan is substantially the same as that of replacing one, the operations will be described together. A damaged and leaking WC pan should never be patched up, since the leakage can be a serious health and hygiene threat. The old pan should be removed.

The soil-pipe collar may be an all-plastic system with a rubber 'O' ring outlet, or fitted into a glazed pipe with tarred hemp and mortar. It is easier to remove the pan connected to a plastic soil system. After unscrewing the pan from the floor, the rubber cone covering the joint can simply be pulled back to allow the pan outlet to be removed. Where an 's' bend pan is connected to a vitreous glazed pipe, great care should be taken not to damage this outlet in the process of removal.

The best way is to break out the old pan at the bend, taking care not to put stress on the collar of the soil pipe. Stuff rag into the collar to stop débris falling in once the pan is removed and then carefully chip away the segments of the pan at the collar joint.

These joints usually consist of a tarred hemp gasket wrapped round the pipe between the socket and the spigot. The joint is completed with a mortar fillet, usually of fast-setting cement. The joint for the new pan can be made using similar materials. The hemp is wrapped tightly round the pipe and pushed well home. Take care not to allow loose ends to intrude into the pipe as a blockage could result.

Where a model of WC suite brings the position of the pan forward of the one replaced, extension pieces, either in plastic or in vitreous glazed pipe or china can be mortared in or connected, with rubber sealing rings as appropriate. The modern push-fit plastic and rubber connectors are simple to fit and have the virtue of being easy to remove if this is necessary.

Another type of plastic connector, available from various manufacturers, enables a quick-fit connection to be made between the pan outlet and the soil-pipe, with a screw-in stem and a rubber outlet seal.

When fitting a new WC pan on solid floor, bed it on to a thick screed of mortar; check first that it is level and allow the mortar to dry before checking finally for firmness. Use a spirit level to check the level of the pan again; small timber wedges can be slid beneath to level up any irregularities. A WC pan has screw-fixing holes through the base. Never screw directly into these or you may crack it. Use brass screws, which will not corrode or rust and set these into rubber grommets. Screw down evenly and check that the pan is firm and again free from movement—avoid overtightening; the pan must never rock or joints might crack and become unseated.

There is no special skill involved in fitting or changing a toilet seat. The only tools needed are a spanner and a screwdriver. There are three basic types of fixing, all of which are through the pre-made holes in the back of the pan. Differences are only of detail of fixing to the seat. Instructions would be supplied with a replacement WC or seat.

71

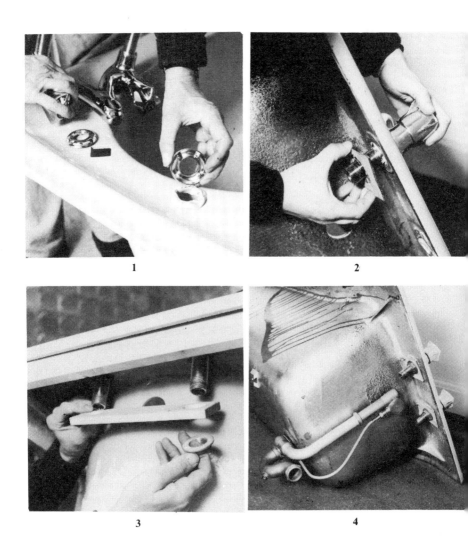

BATHS

1. Bath tap is bedded in plumber's mastic

2. Large rubber washer fitting on bath-tap tail

3. Glass-fibre baths may have wood reinforcing stiffener

4. One type of integrated overflow outlet

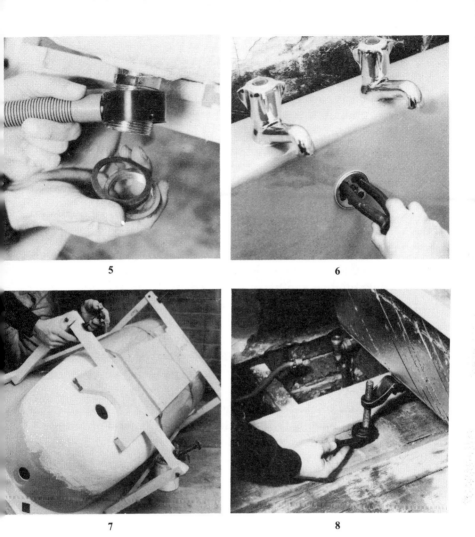

5

6

7

8

5. This overflow connection is in the form of a collar which goes around the waste fitting. The latter has a slot in the side to admit overflow water

6. Tightening overflow outlet by means of ends of pair of pliers

7. Glass-fibre bath with timber reinforcing cradle

8. Baths can be levelled by adjusting the feet

BATHS

Statistics suggest that enamelled cast-iron baths are still the most widely used. Enamelled pressed-steel baths, the next in popularity, are much lighter and, therefore, easier to transport and fit in position. These, however, lack the heat-retaining properties of cast-iron. Acrylic plastic is gaining in popularity as a bath material, although it suffers from a somewhat unfair reputation of being easily scratched and marked. If this happens, it is fairly easy to remove a scratch with fine wire wool, using metal polish to restore the polished surface.

Plastic and steel baths are usually fitted with a cradle support. However, some plastic baths, with ribbed supports, do not require cradling. Modern baths have levelling devices which enables the bath to 'sit' correctly on the floor. Older baths need wedges under the appropriate feet if the floor is not level.

Taps, waste outlet trap and overflow are fitted using similar techniques as for a wash-basin. With pressed steel and plastic baths, the thinner structure necessitates the use of spacing pieces between the tap and the underside of the bath. These accommodate the square shoulders or lugs under the tap body, helping the tap to lock into the correct position.

Combination wastes and overflows are becoming widely used in place of the separate termination of these. The most common has a flexible hose between the overflow and the slotted waste outlet. These are simply fixed, using jointing compound and plastic washers.

Once the bath is in position, use a spirit level to ensure that it is level; this then automatically creates the correct fall for draining.

Keep the rim of the bath as close as possible to the wall. This enables bath sealing, with trim or with mastic, to be carried out effectively.

SHOWERS

It is not so many years ago that a shower unit was considered a luxury in most homes, but today this is no longer the case and many people consider a shower a 'must'. There is a wide variety of showers and shower fittings available. These range from modest, but efficient, attachments for existing bath fittings to factory-made, ready-to-assemble or assembled units. Often seemingly wasted spaces such as deep cupboards or the recesses under stairs can be utilised as shower rooms. Obviously the actual siting of the shower cubicle must be dependent on favourably positioned water supply and drain outlets.

Apart from providing an extra 'bathroom', the shower has many advantages over the more usual 'sit-down' bath. It

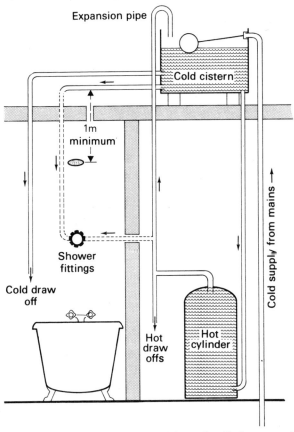

To function correctly, a shower must have a minimum 'head' of pressure of between 910mm–1m. This diagram shows a typical arrangement for a shower.

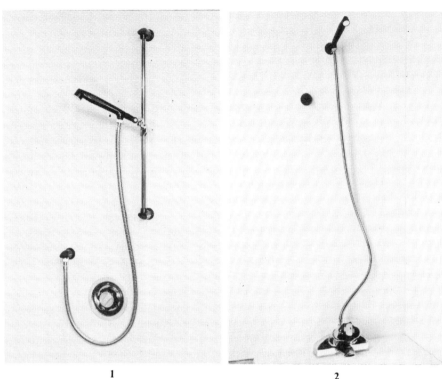

1   2

3

SHOWERS

1. Miraflo shower on slide bar allows adjustment of height and of horizontal projection from wall

2. Walker Crossweller Mira 10 bath/shower combination unit

3. Close up of typical control for shower on bath-tap fitting

4. Mira shower, with bracket which can be set to choice of height and used as a fixed or hand shower. Background: Styles stainless-steel tiles

5. A plastic 'go-anywhere' shower cubicle by Osprey Industries Ltd

takes less space, uses less water and gives the possibility of washing in a continual flow of clean water. Showering also takes less time than a conventional bath. Older people, or those with physical handicaps find them safer—there is not the fear of slipping as there is when getting in and out of a bath.

A shower attachment fitted to a bath mixing set allows the flow of water to be directed either to the bath or shower head. To prevent the entire bathroom being sprayed with water the area around the shower attachment is enclosed. This enclosure is usually effected by using plastic curtaining, suspended on rails at ceiling height, which hangs down inside the bath.

More sophisticated and very popular is the shower cubicle. This consists of three fixed sides with a curtain at the fourth, opening, side. On more expensive units, the fourth side may be in the form of an opening glass door.

As they have to withstand the effects of water and steam the interior walls of the shower cubicle must be of materials

4

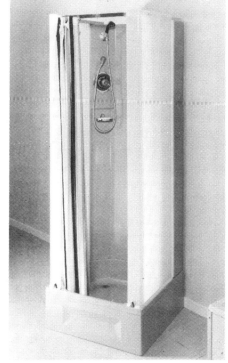

that are waterproof. Most conventional walling and partitional materials are suitable, provided they are themselves waterproof or have a waterproof surface. For this reason ceramic tiles or plastic surfaces are often a popular choice. There is such a wide choice of tiling finishes available today that one has the opportunity to make the shower cubicle an integrated décor feature.

It is important to remember, though, that the grouting must be waterproof. Grouting is the material used for filling the gaps between the tiles. If the surface is not completely waterproof, there is a danger of water seepage getting behind the tiling, causing the surface to lift and crack.

Factory-made shower units usually cost more to buy. They are made of plastic and have the advantage of being light, and easy to install.

In a shower cubicle it is vital to include a tray or upstand to receive the water. The usual method is to use pre-cast trays of plastic or more usually of fireclay. The trays incorporate a waste outlet which can be connected to a trap. The tray is placed in position before putting up the cubicle.

It is quite easy to make a shower tray by laying down a good sand-and-cement mix. The surface is trowelled smooth to close up the pores of the mixture and can later be tiled. Provision should be made for access to the waste outlet, which in some situations will need to be of the shallow-seal trap variety because of space limitations.

Having achieved a smooth surface one has to remember that for old or infirm people it is advisable to have some form of matting, a wooden platform or even a bench seat, as the smooth bottom of a tray can be very slippery.

When showering one wants an even flow of water maintained at a comfortable temperature. Therefore, a method of mixing hot and cold water is necessary.

The usual method of intermingling the flow from the hot and cold supply is to use a mixing set. This allows one to adjust the flow of hot and cold water through the use of two valves or screw-down type taps. If you are using this type of unit it is advisable to set the water flow before entering the cubicle. Firstly open the cold supply and then gradually turn on the hot supply until you have the required temperature and spray force. If there is a fluctuation of pressure to the supply pipes this can affect the mixture setting and possibly result in a scalding for the user.

Thermostatic mixing valves are by far the safest, but also the most expensive of mixing units. They are not dependent on separate supplies but are better given 'first-pull' facilities on the system. The temperature settings are maintained regardless of fluctuations of pressure. Most units have a separate control—usually on the same mounting—which allows the spray force to be varied by the user.

Mixing valves operate similarly to mixing sets and thermostatic mixing valves—except that the water mixing and temperature settings are controlled through a single regulator unit. The same danger from fluctuating pressure applies to the mixing valve as to the mixing set. Only the thermostatic mixing valve overcomes this problem.

The most usual type of shower head closely resembles the spray head fitted to a watering can. With this 'rose'-type head, a pleasant and invigorating spray of water is achieved by forcing the flow of water through many small holes in the headplate.

Another type of head known as the spray-type produces an extremely forceful spray of water. Here the water droplets are atomised by centrifugal force. For this unit to operate satisfactorily a minimum head of 2.44 m (8 ft) is required. It is usually possible to adjust the spray force on these units.

Rose-type heads require a minimum of 910 mm (3 ft) head of water to give a reasonable delivery, though 1.20 m (4 ft) to 1.50 m (5 ft) will provide a more forceful spray. Where it is contemplated installing a shower in an upstairs room, it may be difficult to provide this water head, and this head requirement should be first carefully checked.

The cold-water storage cistern is usually located on the ceiling joists immediately above the first-floor rooms. To achieve the water head required the cistern should be raised on a platform to achieve a minimum distance between the cistern base and the shower head—the highest fixing point on adjustable fittings—of not less than 910 mm (3 ft). If the pipe run to the shower is long or there are a number of bends to be negotiated the platform should be raised slightly higher to compensate for and overcome the resistance created.

Most shower units require 15 mm ($\frac{1}{2}$ in) supplies, though some need 22 mm ($\frac{3}{4}$ in) to maintain an adequate water force. If bends in the pipe are hampering supply or the pipes are scaled, a 22 mm supply branch to the shower where it can be reduced to 15 mm may provide a solution.

Supplies of hot and cold water to a shower unit should always be of equal pressure. Cold supplies must be taken from the cold-water storage cistern. Water authorities forbid the cold supply to be taken from the rising main, and the same applies for baths.

If the hot- and cold-water mixing fittings are of the non-thermostatic type it is a good practice to take two separate supplies to the shower unit. In cases where two separate supplies are not feasible try to see that the shower supplies have 'first pull' on the distribution supplies. Sudden demand from draw-off points can cause dangerous fluctuations of pressure.

If the hot-water supply is reduced you may only have the pleasure of an invigorating cold shower but if the cold supply is lacking there is a real risk of severe scalding. Serious though this would be for anyone, to an old person or a young child it could prove fatal. Therefore, a little care spent installing separate supplies could ensure safety and peace of mind.

Testing all installations before final concealment or boxing-in of pipework is most important. Where possible it looks much neater to conceal all pipework. Many shower fitments provide for hidden supplies. It is possible to chase wall surfaces and sink in pipes, or they can be boxed in behind the shower walling. It is wise, however, to make maintenance possible by fitting removable panels or removable tiled sections. Chromium-plated tubing greatly enhances the appearance of pipework that has to be seen.

WATER HEATERS

ELECTRIC HEATERS

There are four main types of electric water and storage heaters. These usually consist of a copper cylinder enclosed by an enamelled steel casing.

'Free-outlet' or single-point heaters supply hot water to one particular place, though it may be possible to serve two adjacent points by using a swivel-arm arrangement. The most popular sizes have a capacity of 7 litres (about $1\frac{1}{2}$ gallons) or 14 litres (3 gallons). These are suitable for use at kitchen sinks or wash-hand basins where there is no alternative hot-water supply or the hot-water source is so far away that a long draw off from the hot-water storage cylinder would be wasteful. It is possible to obtain 'free-outlet' type heaters in sizes of up to 91 litres (20 gallons).

Where the appliance is fitted over a kitchen sink, it may be preferable to draw the cold supply from the mains, but supply can also be taken from the cold-water storage cistern. The local water authority should be informed of any proposals to connect direct to mains. The heater works on the principle that cold water enters at the bottom of the cylinder, causing hot water at the top to spill out over the weir-type outlet. The expansion of hot water is allowed for in the design.

A second type of low-pressure electric water heater has a similar pipe layout to the conventional hot-water cylinder. Cold water drawn from the cold-storage cistern is raised in temperature by an immersion heater and then vented back to the cold-water storage cistern through a draw-off pipe. It is possible to have several draw-off points along the pipe run. Low-pressure heaters cannot be connected to the mains and must be supplied from the cold storage cistern.

Some models are fitted with two immersion heaters, one in the upper section to supply hand basins, and the other in the lower section working in conjunction with the first to supply hot water at times of greater demand such as wash day, bath time and so on. Both heaters then heat the full contents of the unit. It is possible to have floor- or wall-mounted low-pressure heaters.

Another type of heater is the combination unit, used ideally where no hot water system already exists or head-room limitations prevent the use of an independent cold-water storage cistern. It is usually more economic to install than a conventional system because it incorporates its own cold-water storage. For this reason, it must be situated above the highest draw-off point, otherwise the necessary head of water will be lacking.

The combination unit is a dual-purpose appliance consisting of an upper cold-water cistern and a lower hot-water section, connected by a supply pipe leading to the bottom of the hot-water section. A vent pipe, rising from the bottom of the top section, allows for hot water expansion. With a conventional overflow connection from the cold-water section, all that is needed to complete the self-contained combination is a cold feed which enters via a ball valve from either the mains or a further storage cistern. An independent source of heat can be fitted in the form of an immersion heater, or any other water heating method can be used via the flow and return pipes.

When fitting a combination unit, it is always wise to use one with an adequate capacity. If you fit one unable to cope with the maximum demand you may have problems, and when a large amount of water is drawn off—say for a bath or filling a washing machine—the low-capacity cold-water section may be emptied. This can be remedied by reducing the flow of hot water to allow the cold feed to keep up, or by anticipating this problem and increasing the size of the unit, also leaving a safety margin. Combination units can be used with indirect hot-water systems.

1. Creda Corvette electric 2.5 kW keater, capacity around 4.55 litres (1 gallon) of water. The transparent flask enables you to see the water level

2. The Ascot 20.25 gas bulk-storage heater is available in conventional-flue and balanced-flue versions

3. The Ascot 527 is available as a single- or multi-point heater. It is finished in brushed stainless steel

4. A gas circulator, operating on town or natural gas, the Ascot 305C

1

2

3

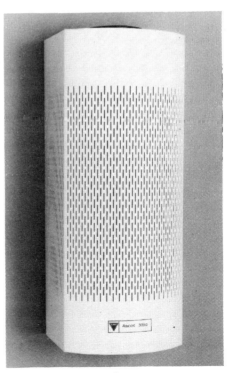

4

Working on the same principle as the combination unit is the cistern type of electric water heater. These cistern heaters are meant to be seen and are usually encased in enamelled steel jackets. In some models the hot-water section is insulated, as is the wall between the hot and cold sections. Heating is by an immersion heater and the hot water can be drawn in any part of the house. A wide selection of models is produced to suit the varied demands of particular household requirements.

A fourth type of electric water heater that does not use storage principles is known as an instantaneous water heater. The incoming cold water flows over plates containing electrical elements. These heat the water, the flow being regulated according to the temperature of the water that is required. Such heaters cannot provide the full supply of a storage heater, but for localised hot water at a given point they are very effective. Used as heaters for showers or handbasins they have many advantages. Most models can be run directly off the cold main—with Water Board approval—or from a storage cistern, provided there is a sufficient head of water. In either case only one supply pipe is needed, making installation cheaper. The necessary power is supplied by a 13 amp socket. The fact that you only heat the water you are going to use, and that you do not have the heat losses of a storage heater, makes this form of water heating highly competitive in running costs. There is no wide difference in the initial purchase price between an instantaneous heater and a storage heaters.

GAS HEATERS

Gas-fired heaters can be divided into two types—storage and instantaneous. Very popular is the storage heater with the circulator boiler connected to a hot-water cylinder. The water heats in the boiler and is transferred to the storage cylinder via a circulating pipe. Another pipe draws cooler water from the base of the cylinder back to the boiler to be reheated. This system is similar to the normal flow-and-return domestic heating and hot-water arrangement.

Gas appliances emit fumes, and some means of removing these must be provided. This is often achieved by means of an asbestos flue-pipe taken through an exterior wall. Many gas circulators are coupled directly to a hot-water cylinder and the flue pipe is taken out through a rear wall. Most of these units are thermostatically controlled.

Instantaneous gas water heaters can be single or multi-point. Again, subject to Water Board consent, both can be run off the mains cold supply or from a cold-water storage cistern which provides a good water head. A wide range of appliances is available and it is well worth investigating the different types of heater so as to find the one best suited to your requirements.

At a kitchen sink or wash-hand basin, a single-point instantaneous gas heater is a good choice. If it is connected to the cold main the hot water can be used for cooking; you cannot use water drawn from a hot cylinder for this purpose. One model is designed to supply water at temperatures varying from boiling to hot or warm, this being achieved by fitting hot and cold taps and a three-position temperature selector.

There are also gas-fired heaters which will supply hot water at several points in the house. When a hot tap is turned on the water flow opens the main gas supply, which is ignited by the pilot light. A safety device prevents the main gas supply from coming on when the pilot is not alight, With instantaneous heaters plumbing is minimized as they require no expansion allowance.

Some heaters can be semi-recessed. Fresh air for combustion is drawn in from the outside of the house via an incorporated, room-sealed duct—thus allowing the working parts of the unit to be let into the wall. Some units project as little as 130 mm (5 in) from the wall.

GARDEN TAPS

A garden tap is a valuable asset. However, it needs to work under pressure to meet the need of any average garden hose, and the supply from the storage system is frequently not great enough to give the desired pressure through any long run of hose. Standard water regulations stipulate that only one appliance may be connected directly to rising mains; this is usually the kitchen cold-water service, which thus also has the advantage of being a fresh-water supply. Nevertheless, the outside tap is frequently fed from the rising main, and a dispensation to connect this should be obtained from the local water authority.

The connection normally requires only a short section of pipework and a suitable tee connection in the main supply pipe. Frequently the garden tap is located outside the kitchen, enabling the pipe to be taken through the wall. This can be done with a long-reach drill bit in an 19 mm or $\frac{3}{4}$ in electric power drill, or an electric rotary hammer. As an alternative to these special tools, a medium cold chisel and club hammer can equally be used.

When making holes through walls, avoid going completely through from one side; this will probably break out a large chunk of brickwork. Stop when nearly through, measure to find the corresponding position on the other side and complete the hole from there.

Outdoor taps are available with threaded nozzles so that locking rings can be used to make firm hose connections.

It is important to insulate outside taps. A good way to do this is to make a simple wooden casing and to line this with glass fibre or some other insulating material. The box can be made removable and only put in position during winter months.

ABOUT DRAINAGE

Domestic drainage may be said to fall into two categories—that above ground and that below ground. The system above ground consists of pipework from sinks, WC's, baths, gutters and the like; below ground are the services collectively known as 'drains'.

Appliances discharging into the drainage system are fitted with traps which act as water seals, preventing foul air from percolating back into the home. These fall into two categories: the tubular and the bottle trap. There are shallow- and deep-seal versions. Traps have a tubular plug or a detachable bottle to facilitate the removal of blockages.

WC pans terminate in two types of trap, the 'p' trap and the 's' trap, each resembling the appropriate letter of the alphabet. Traps connecting kitchen and bathroom waste to the main drainage—called the soil system—are known as trapped yard gullies. These have a 'u' bend which maintains the necessary permanent water seal.

Modern building regulations prescribe that main pipes connecting baths, toilets and basins to the drains—normally with a diameter of 102 mm (4 in)—must be located inside the structure of the house. While this presents a less unsightly external appearance, the rule was introduced as a safeguard against the freezing up of these pipes in cold weather.

Some means are necessary for venting sewage gases to the atmosphere. As the water-seal in traps prevents the gases permeating the home, these are normally vented through a pipe positioned about 1 m above the highest window, or where there is no possibility of permeation.

Many older houses have a two-pipe plumbing system consisting of separate waste and soil services. The waste services are frequently fed into a hopper and often to a trapped yard gully and thence to a manhole. In the modern single-pipe system, all, or nearly all, services are connected to the soil pipe by means of branch fittings. Exceptions are made for certain ground-floor connections, for example a separate WC on another side of the house, and waste from the kitchen sink and domestic kitchen appliances, which drain to the trapped yard gully.

Current building regulations do not allow the older, two-pipe system to be used in new housing. The single-pipe system also reduces the amount of pipework used. One problem it creates, however, is that of siphonage. This is where the use of one appliance sucks the water seal from the trap of another, allowing noxious gases to enter the house. It can also be caused where two appliances are joined to one waste outlet connected to the soil pipe—a practice to be avoided, unless siphonage is overcome by the use of anti-siphon pipes, which supply air to the appliance and prevent water from being sucked out. In the single-stack system, the vent pipe stops siphonage at the same time as providing ventilation.

SINGLE-STACK SYSTEM

The single-stack system relies on one pipe for soil, waste and venting. However, for this to be possible, the pipe layout must conform with strict design requirements and the trap seals must also be 76 mm (3 in) deep.

First, the junction between the stack pipe and the drain must consist of a long-radius bend and not be a sharp knuckle, as on some older systems. This helps to keep the fluids moving at an even rate and lessens the chances of back pressure at the lowest branch. The vertical distance between the lowest branch on the main stack and the bottom, or 'invert', of the drain should not be less than 760 mm (2 ft 6 in).

All soil branch connections to the stack must be swept in the direction of the flow. To avoid suction, there must be no branch connection closer than 200 mm (8 in) below the entry of a WC branch. Hand-basin traps should be of the 'p' pattern, which is less susceptible to siphonage than the 's' type. Bath and sink traps should have 'p' traps connected and waste pipes should be short and sloped as gently as possible.

Many existing soil pipes are made of cast iron. If this becomes fractured, the section should be removed and no

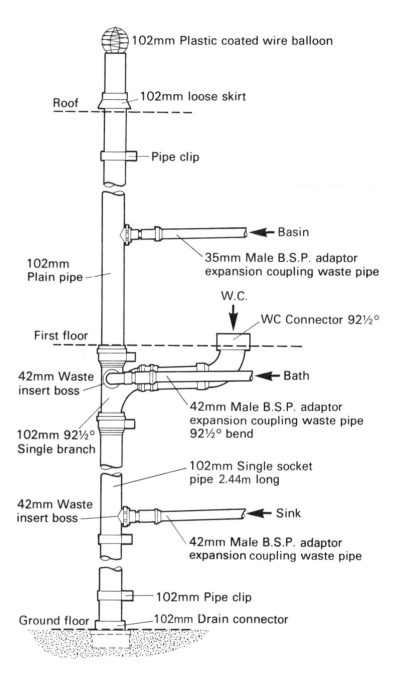

102mm Plastic coated wire balloon

102mm loose skirt

Roof

Pipe clip

Basin

35mm Male B.S.P. adaptor
expansion coupling waste pipe

102mm
Plain pipe

W.C.

WC Connector 92½°

First floor

42mm Waste
insert boss

Bath

42mm Male B.S.P. adaptor
expansion coupling waste pipe
92½° bend

102mm 92½°
Single branch

102mm Single socket
pipe 2.44m long

42mm Waste
insert boss

Sink

42mm Male B.S.P. adaptor
expansion coupling waste pipe

102mm Pipe clip

Ground floor

102mm Drain connector

Semi or detached single stack soil and drainage system ('S' trap pan) attempt should be made to patch it up.

Cast iron pipes slot together and the joint is consolidated by either a mixture of red lead and putty or a proprietary mastic. The joint is given a final surfacing of bitumen mastic.

The pipes are fixed to walls, and these are usually plugged and the pipes secured by clips at each joint, fastened on with pipe nails. To remove a damaged section, the nails can usually be pulled out with a claw hammer to release the clip. This releases the pipe and the damaged section can then be removed easily. To replace a full section of pipe, two sets of clips may have to be removed. Take care to support any 'floating' lengths of pipe. When replacing a section of pipe, one should also replace the old wall plugs with new timber wedges or proprietary plugs.

If the section to be replaced is at ground level, the connection is probably into the socket end of a salt-glazed sewer pipe. The collar will be mortared, and this fillet should be

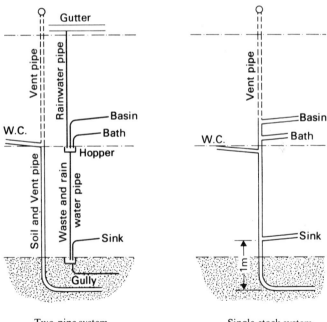

Two-pipe system Single-stack system

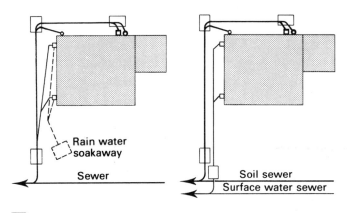

Rain water
soakaway

Sewer

Soil sewer

Surface water sewer

☐ Inspection chamber
▫ Rain water gully
● Vent pipe
◻ Waste gully
○ Soil pipe

Plan of domestic soil and stormwater drainage

gently chipped away with a sharp cold chisel, to clear the pipe, which can then be removed.

A plumb bob should be used to establish vertical alignment with the pipes temporarily slotted together so that the brackets are accurately positioned, to enable the sections to join correctly.

When the new section is replaced, secure this firmly to the wall with its clips, having first carefully lined the pipe up with the salt-glazed socket. A tarred-rope gasket seal should be made at the joint and a new collar of mortar should be applied using a stiff 1:4 cement-sand mix.

A similar procedure applies when replacing any branch section to a WC which may be joined to a section of salt-glazed pipe.

PLASTIC SOIL PIPE

In many cases, it may pay to renew the old pipework with a new plastic system. PVC, in common with all plastics, has a high rate of thermal expansion and this should be adequately and correctly accommodated. Seal-ring joints accommodate thermal expansion, enabling solvent welds to be used elsewhere in the system.

Unless each fitting and expansion point is firmly anchored, accumulative movement or escalation can take place, and the whole installation can become dimensionally unstable. This can lead, particularly on horizontal runs, to joints actually pulling apart. Clips and fixings should be carefully aligned to ensure longitudinal freedom.

To cut a plastic pipe squarely, use a fine-tooth saw. Mark the position of the cut to be made, double checking that this is correct, and wrap a newspaper round the pipe, bringing its edges together, on the line of the cut. Cut to this template and the result should then be square.

Caulking rings enable salt-glazed pipe to be connected to PVC pipe. This should be solvent-welded to the foot of the stack pipe and the collar is then mortared in the conventional way. A connector also enables PVC pipe to be connected to pitch fibre, and cast-iron to be joined to PVC pipe.

Pipes laid underground should be below the 'frost line', though there is no recorded instance of damage to underground PVC pipe, even in exceptionally severe conditions.

Connectors are also made for joining PVC pipes to metal fittings. Jointing is usually by screw fittings, using ptfe tape to seal and lubricate the thread. Other items include tank and cistern connectors, adaptors, reducing bushes, tap connectors, unions and stopcock and gate valves—in fact, a full range of domestic plumbing fittings.

Similarly, adaptors are available to join plastic waste pipe to cast-iron pipe, where internal plumbing is modernized with plastic but existing cast-iron stack pipe is retained.

Where a vent pipe is taken through a roof opening, various possibilities exist for sealing the join. The most common is a

1. Fixing soil pipe holderbat into wall of house

2. Ventilator goes into 'O'-ring seal. Note swanneck used to clear plastic roof gutter (both Key Terrain Ltd)

3. Conventional mortaring of a vitreous glazed pipe

4. Trapped yard gulley fitted into drain outlet

5. Soil drainage system using plastic manhole and pipework (Osma Plastics Ltd)

1

2

3

4

5

weathering apron, part of a pre-formed roof outlet assembly. Fittings are available for connection through asphalt and mineral-felt surfaces, and for screeded finishes on balconies. Fixing methods depend on the make of product and fixing instructions should be followed for these.

Holderbats or pipe-fixing clips may be fixed to walls with washered drive nails. On some makes, a special tool is available for fixing the nails into the masonry. Washered drive screws can also be used.

Branch boss adaptors for connecting wastes, giving the correct degree of fall ($1\frac{1}{4}°$), can be fitted to pipe where required. It is possible to fit a section with bosses and branches already incorporated, but later adaption or extension of the system is more easily carried out by cutting the soil pipe and fitting a boss. Some pipe sections are fitted with the boss stem and merely have to have the centre cut out with a hole cutter. Some fittings can be solvent welded to the boss; others are fitted with a lock nut with 'o' ring seal.

Usually a boss is fitted by means of a solvent weld. First, the hole has to be drilled. A hole or radius cutter is the usual tool, though a pilot hole can be drilled and a hole saw used to cut the required aperture. Similarly, an access door or inspection hatch can be located in a stack pipe by cutting two parallel holes, one below the other, and enlarging this to an oblong shape with a file.

It is important to clean all solvent from the holes in the connection to the stack pipe as this could cause obstruction in the pipe by impeding the smooth flow of waste.

Access doors are either fixed to the pipe with a pipe clamp or fitted into the pipe and locked in place by a centre screw which expands the fitting laterally. This, again, depends on the makes.

CUTTING AND CONNECTING DRAINAGE

Drainage pipes are made in varying lengths but sometimes have to be cut to fit the chosen layout.

Pipes in cast iron, plastic or asbestos cement can be cut with a hacksaw, though a sheet saw is easier for cutting cast-

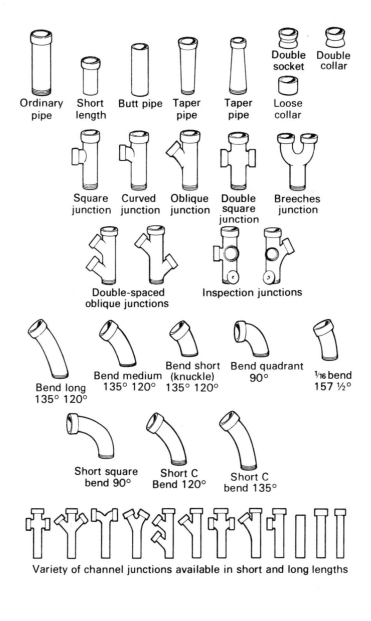

Ordinary pipe · Short length · Butt pipe · Taper pipe · Taper pipe · Double socket · Double collar · Loose collar

Square junction · Curved junction · Oblique junction · Double square junction · Breeches junction

Double-spaced oblique junctions · Inspection junctions

Bend long 135° 120° · Bend medium 135° 120° · Bend short (knuckle) 135° 120° · Bend quadrant 90° · ¹⁄₁₆ bend 157 ½°

Short square bend 90° · Short C Bend 120° · Short C bend 135°

Variety of channel junctions available in short and long lengths

Branch bends ¾ and ½ section

Kitchen sink gulley

Interceptor

Examples of types of glazed pipework

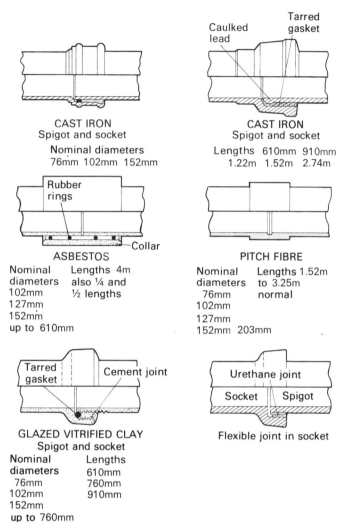

CAST IRON
Spigot and socket
Nominal diameters
76mm 102mm 152mm

Caulked lead

Tarred gasket

CAST IRON
Spigot and socket
Lengths 610mm 910mm
1.22m 1.52m 2.74m

Rubber rings

ASBESTOS
Collar

Nominal diameters	Lengths 4m
102mm	also ¼ and
127mm	½ lengths
152mm	
up to 610mm	

PITCH FIBRE

Nominal diameters	Lengths 1.52m
76mm	to 3.25m
102mm	normal
127mm	
152mm 203mm	

Tarred gasket

Cement joint

GLAZED VITRIFIED CLAY
Spigot and socket

Nominal diameters	Lengths
76mm	610mm
102mm	760mm
152mm	910mm
up to 760mm	

Urethane joint

Socket   Spigot

Flexible joint in socket

Types of joint used with a variety of pipe materials

iron pipe. With pitch fibre an ordinary handsaw is best. The cut should be lubricated with water to prevent the tar in the pipe's material from clogging the teeth.

Clay, or glazed vitreous pipe, can be cut successfully, but care and patience are necessary. Once the cut position has been marked completely round the pipe, the pipe is packed

A. Open gulley with grating. For outside use to take surface water only.

B. Sealed gulley, similar to open but with cover over inlet sealed. For outside use for waste and rainwater.

C. Access gulley. Used when it can replace additional manhole. Second cover for rodding drain yard gulley has screw-down access cover.

D. Back-inlet gulley. Vertical inlet designed to take rainwater and waste water. Various inlet positions.

E. Various positions of inlet diagonal positions are available, as well as combinations.

F. Trap with raising piece and horizontal inlet.

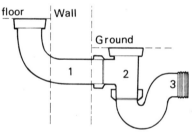

G. 1. Long-arm bend
   2. Raising piece with horizontal inlet.
   3. 'P' trap.

Gulleys and traps

with sand and laid on sand or soft earth. A hammer and a small, sharp cold chisel are used to break the glaze or surface completely round the pipe.

Continue the cut round the pipe, progressively deepening this. Use only gentle blows, to avoid breaking the pipe. When the pipe is about to part, the ringing sound made by the blows will deepen to a thud. Carefully continue chipping until the two parts separate.

Clay pipes can be joined in two ways—with a rigid connection and with a flexible joint. The first method is more traditional. The spigot end of a pipe is introduced into the socket of another. A tarred rope gasket is wrapped around the spigot. The joints should be well pushed together, so that no rope protrudes into the pipe, as this could lead to blockage and probably a poor and leaky joint.

The gasket should be compressed into the socket for about one third of its depth, using a blunt chisel or similar tool to push it well home. The joint is surfaced with a 1:3 cement-sand mix, trowelled around and into the joint. Mortar must also not be allowed to intrude into the pipe.

Cover the finished joints with wet sacking overnight and, next morning, apply a final smooth collar of mortar. This allows for shrinkage of the first application of mortar. It is important that such connections are not disturbed once they are made. Finally, cover these joints again for about another twelve hours with wet sacking.

'Mechanical' joints are now preferred to the rigid variety. These use rubber gaskets and 'o' rings and can be used for cast-iron, concrete, vitrified clay and asbestos-cement pipe. A special lubricant used on internal surfaces helps insertion and the joint forms a watertight seal.

Pitch-fibre pipes, originally joined by driving tapered pipe ends together in a collar, are now much more simply joined with a ring-seal. The older method involved the use of a special lathe to cut the tapered joints. Joints can be made to pitch fibre and most other materials by means of special connectors, to both rainwater and soil systems. Complete soil systems can be built of pitch fibre and related polypropylene fittings. A range of slipper bends are made which can be used with pitch fibre or other drainage systems. Complete system details are available from manufacturers of this product, such as Key Terrain Ltd, of Larkfield, Kent.

Plastic pipes can be joined in two ways—either by the ring-seal method or by cement welding. The method of welding is similar to that used to join smaller pipes and the pipe should be similarly prepared. With these larger pipes, two people are needed, since the welding solvent goes off quickly. One needs to apply the solvent and the other to make the joint.

Cast-iron pipes are often used under concrete sub-floors, though plastic pipe is now accepted by many local authorities in this context. Older jointing methods used lead caulking between socket and spigot on cast-iron pipes. However, joints, can now be made with socketless pipes, using a flexible coupling. One type uses a collar and a rubber ring on each pipe end, which is then pushed into a sleeve. Bolts are inserted through the collars and compress the rings to seal the joint.

REPAIRS TO PIPE RUNS

In fairly deep trenches, the sides should be shored to prevent collapse of the walls. If a vitreous pipe is fractured, you will need to 'spring' out that pipe and the pipe on either side of it —a total of three pipes. On flexibly jointed pipes, it is not possible to use the 'springing' technique; you will have to cut or carefully break the damaged section. If, however, the collar of a pipe section becomes broken or damaged, this can be neatly trimmed back to the body of the pipe, using the technique described earlier for cutting glazed pipes, and a stoneware double collar can be fitted, using a tarred-rope gasket and mortar or the ring-seal method to effect the joint.

BEDDING PIPES

A minimum depth of 100 mm of compacted granular material, such as broken stone or gravel, 5 mm to 10 mm in size, should form the basis of a trench. Material should not ideally exceed 20 mm in size. Indentations should be made in this base so that the pipe sockets bed in and the pipe body is not left 'floating'.

The backfill should consist of selected excavated material from which stones larger than 25 mm and lumps of clay have been removed. It should be carefully compacted in layers about 100 mm to 300 mm thick above the crown of the pipe. The remainder should be placed in 300 mm thick layers to give a total cover of 600 mm above the crown of the pipe for normal circumstances.

INTERCEPTORS

In older drainage systems, interceptors are fitted to the outlet side of the last inspection chamber. These provide a water seal between the main sewer and the domestic drainage. The interceptor, shaped somewhat like a Grecian urn, has a stopper which, when removed, enables rodding to be carried out between this outlet and the main sewer.

The interceptor presents a possible blockage point, and in much new building it is dispensed with, venting being effected corporately by venting arrangements in the various holds.

CONNECTION TO PUBLIC SEWERS

This is carried out by or under the supervision of the local authority. It involves fixing a 'saddle' connector to the main sewer, to connect the domestic sewer service. While local authorities may permit a private householder to open up the highway, under licence, to lay drain services, they usually insist on making the saddle connections themselves.

Where a highway is opened, at least half the carriageway must be left free to traffic. Warning lights and obstruction indication must also be given. The authority's Clerk of Works will normally supervise the opening of a highway and the reinstatement of the roadway. Once replacement soil has been well tamped down, the authority will retarmac and otherwise reinstate the surface. A charge is levied for this and for connection of the drain services to the main sewer.

10

MANHOLES AND HOW TO MAINTAIN THEM

Among the least attractive of garden 'ornaments' is the manhole lid—or inspection-chamber cover, to give it its correct title. This 'puts the lid' on an essential safeguard to health in modern living, for beneath the cover is the manhole, or inspection chamber. The manhole—as the name implies —serves to provide access for clearance and periodic maintenance to the pipework system providing for disposal of wastes from the household. Lids may be of cast iron, but steel or aluminium are newer materials.

Drains must be fully watertight and not subject to blockage, and manholes are fitted where any change of direction or gradient is encountered. The standard and usual size of a pipe is a diameter of 102 mm (4 in). There must be a constant fall in the pipe—not too shallow or too steep, since blockages might otherwise occur. The usual gradient is 1 in 40. Where pipework enters the manhole, the branch connections used must be swept in the direction of flow.

Pipework in the inspection chamber is usually of the vitreous glazed variety. Pitch fibre and plastic are among newer materials, and ready-made drains of plastic or concrete can be fitted where manholes need to be rebuilt or a new one fitted. These can save much time and tedious construction work.

The way to deal with blockages is, in severe cases, to rod them with a set of screw together brushes, rather like those used by chimney sweeps. The manhole must therefore be constructed with sufficient room to permit the rodding operation. With shallow manholes, the size need be no larger than the cover, for example: 460 mm × 610 mm (18 in × 24 in).

With drains on a steeply sloping terrain, it is not always possible to preserve consistently the required ratio of fall. Where this happens, a stepped type of intercepting chamber is used. This allows the level to be dropped substantially, while maintaining the desired gradient of fall over the rest of the soil drainage system. This type of manhole is called a back-drop or back-entry inspection chamber. It consists of a pipeline positioned vertically behind the chamber which directs the flow into a bend and into the channel at the bottom of the manhole. Such manholes may be fairly deep and a system of steps should be incorporated into the walls of the manhole to allow access to the bottom.

Rodding is not possible with the vertical, back-drop pipe, but a rodding point should be incorporated near the top of the chamber giving access to the horizontal section of the pipe linking with the previous inspection chamber. This is normally sealed with a removable plug, bedded in bitumen.

With deeper manholes, the size must be increased to allow for easy working access. The chart below gives the relative sizes for manholes at various depths. The depth is taken from the bottom of the pipe, known as the 'invert'.

Depth to invert	Length	Width	Thickness of wall
up to 610 mm (2 ft)	610 mm (2 ft)	460 mm (1 ft 6 in)	114 mm (4½ in)
610 mm to 910 mm (2 ft–3 ft)	737 mm (2 ft 5 in)	572 mm (1 ft 10¼ in)	114 mm (4½ in)
910 mm to 1.53 m (3 ft–6 ft)	1.02 m (3 ft 4¼ in)	686 mm (2 ft 3 in)	229 mm (9 in)
1.83 m to 4.57 mm (6 ft–15 ft)	1.37 mm (4 ft 6 in)	798 mm (2 ft 7¼ in)	229 mm (9 in)

(Note: brick sizes have not yet been standardized in a metric (SI) module, and the conversions are metric equivalent of the imperial.)

The concrete base should be of the same size as the external dimensions of the chamber and at least 150 mm thick. Channels in the base may be of half-round glazed or pitch-fibre pipe, or made by using a smooth object such as a tin to form them in the concrete.

The sides of the manhole must be built of dense and non-porous bricks, such as Class B engineering bricks. This type of brick is able to withstand the constant damp conditions that exist below ground. Bricks should be laid in English bond and with the 'frog' (indentation) upwards for maximum strength in a mortar not weaker than 1 : 3 cement to sand. If conventional 'stock' bricks are used, these should be 'parged' or rendered, to provide the same protection as engineering bricks; the latter should not be rendered. Some local authorities will not accept the use of stock bricks.

The concrete base is known as 'benching'. It should be shaped so that it rises from the channel in the centre to the sides of the manhole, at a gradient of about 25 mm : 152 mm (1 in : 6 in). Benching should use a mix of 1 : 4 cement and sharp sand and be finished off with a steel trowel. Benching must be kept clean, and if any cracks appear in it these should be immediately repaired. If this is not done a major rebuild job may be needed once the concrete has had time to break away completely. Brickwork should be inspected at fairly regular intervals and any rendering or pointing which is faulty should be repaired.

Precast concrete manholes should have watertight joints. In waterlogged ground it may be necessary to surround the sections with 150 mm of concrete; take care to pack it under incoming and outgoing pipes.

MANHOLE COVERS

The manhole cover must be kept in top condition to ensure that it maintains the necessary air-tight seal over the system. Where a manhole has to be sited within the house, apart from the cover being completely air-tight, it must, as an extra precaution, be bolted to the frame to ensure that it does not become dislodged. These bolts need to be removable to allow the lid to be removed.

If a manhole cover is broken and has to be replaced, with the cast-iron type you should buy a new rim as well as a lid. These are made as a 'matched pair' and this ensures a good fit. Though a matched cover and rim will fit together tightly they are not machined sufficiently to provide a totally airtight seal. It is, therefore, necessary to apply a liberal coating of manhole grease to the rim before laying the lid in position. If

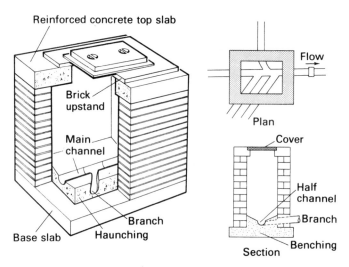

Construction of inspection chamber (manhole)

the lid is removed for inspection it is advisable to remove all old grease and repack it to maintain the seal and prevent dirt from entering the manhole and blocking pipes.

Manhole rims should be set in a concrete surround, making them relatively simple to replace. To remove the rim the surrounding concrete must be chipped away, with a club hammer and small cold chisel. Take care to avoid damaging brickwork below the rim. Where necessary all deterioration in mortar and brickwork should be made good.

Bed the cover frame solidly in a 1 : 3 cement-mortar mix over its whole area to ensure an even bearing. Do this with the lid in position to avoid twisting the frame, and ensure that the cover does not rock. Use a spirit level to ensure accurate alignment.

TESTING

Manholes should be tested continually for an hour, during which there should be no significant loss of water. A fall of more than 25 mm in this time would normally indicate an unreasonable water loss, not accounted for by absorption within the chamber walls and dissipation.

The section of drain should first be isolated and charged

104

with water. This is done by means of drain plugs, which have rubber walls, expanded by means of a screw on the centre of the plug body, to fit into the entry point of the channel. The section can also be drained slowly by unscrewing a nut; the plug can then be fully removed when this has reduced the pressure of water.

BLOCKAGES

Usually where a blockage occurs in an inspection chamber at the entry or outflow points, a stick, carefully used, will be adequate for clearing out the débris. In more severe cases of blockage, you may need a set of drainage rods and fittings. These can be hired from sources such as DIY shops, builders' merchants and hire firms.

In order to find the blockage, begin at the house and open up the inspection chambers in turn. An empty chamber indicates that the blockage is between it and the previous one. Before rodding, put a temporary barrier across the mouth of the outflow pipe in the empty chamber, such as a piece of chicken wire rolled into a ball; this allows the water to pass but stops solid matter. It must be large enough not to enter the pipe.

Rods screw together and are about 1 m (about 3 ft) in length. The rods are reasonably flexible, so that they can be fed in at an angle from outside shallower manholes. The main screw-on cleaning attachments are a rubber plunger, corkscrew head, hook scraper and brush head. The corkscrew is designed to unscrew the blockage.

First, attach the rubber plunger and insert this at the blocked chamber. Always turn the rods in a clock-wise direction as you insert them; this ensures that they do not unscrew. Normally, you will be able to push the obstruction clear. If this fails, the hook scraper and corkscrew are employed. Once débris is dislodged, remove this from the drain and flush it out with a hose; use the brush to clean off any débris.

Finally, carefully inspect the surfacings to find out if any flaw or deterioration is causing the adhesion and building up of waste matter, and correct this if necessary.

11

MAINTENANCE AND FIRST AID

Plumbing systems are, like cars, vacuum cleaners and washing machines, composed of moving parts that from time to time need maintenance and overhaul to keep them running smoothly and efficiently.

DRIPPING TAPS

One of the most irritating faults is that of a dripping tap. Taps give extremely efficient service when you think of the constant use they get. They are, however, one of the most vulnerable parts of any plumbing system. There are two basic types of tap. The bib tap, with its horizontal water inlet, and the more modern vertical-inlet pillar tap.

Both operate on the same principle. When the tap is turned down, the water is prevented by a resilient washer pressed down over the valve seat from flowing from the inlet to the outlet. The washer is attached to a jumper which sits loosely at the base of the spindle, to which the handle is attached. As the handle is turned the spindle rises, allowing water pressure to lift the jumper and a flow to take place. Sometimes the jumper does not 'jump' as it is attached to the spindle by a press fit. This alternative is used when low water pressure would not move the normal type of jumper.

It is the washer which is the weak part of the system. It may become worn, or the valve seat can be partially obstructed with foreign particles which prevent the washer from seating correctly. The result in either event is the familiar drip. Before taking the tap apart, try turning it on fully in order to see if the sudden force of the full flow of water will dislodge the obstructions. If this does not work then the tap will have to be dismantled.

There are two important things to remember before tackling this or any plumbing job. First, always collect together all the materials and tools you need, and second, turn the water supply off before starting the job. The water supply into the house can be turned off at the rising main stopcock —which is usually located under or near the kitchen sink. It is important that everyone knows the whereabouts of the stopcock and how to turn the water off should the need arise. The stopcock should be checked occasionally and the stem greased if necessary, to ensure that it will operate smoothly and quickly in an emergency.

Most often it is the kitchen cold tap which goes faulty, and as this supply comes from the mains, it is the main stopcock which should be turned off. Where the water supply and the tap come from a storage cistern it is better to turn off the water between the tap and the cistern where possible, to make draining the cistern unnecessary. The hot-water taps are usually isolated by turning off the stopcock in the cold-water feed to the hot-water cylinder. If there is no stopcock the whole system must be drained down. To do this, first turn off the stopcock in the rising main just before it enters the cold-water storage cistern or tie up the ball-valve arm, then open all the taps in the house to drain the cistern.

Allow the water to drain off and then remove the tap cover. This should be possible with hand pressure, but if not use a wrench or spanner—first wrapping a cloth round the cover to protect the chromium plating or brass. To facilitate easy removal of the cover next time, smear the threads with petroleum jelly. Once you have lifted the cover you will see the headgear. The hexagonal nut on this should be loosened and the washer will now be exposed on the valve seat—or, if the jumper is of the low-pressure type, it will come out with the spindle.

The jumper is usually made of brass and the washer is secured to it with a brass nut which may seize up. In trying to free it you may distort the jumper, so it is wise to have a spare jumper and washer set. When screwing down the new washer, grease the threads of the nut to facilitate ease of movement. While not all washers are suitable for hot and cold taps, synthetic rubber washers will do for both. An oversized washer can be trimmed.

If the water is by-passing the washer because the valve seat is worn or pitted, this can be reground. It is usually a job best left to a specialist with the necessary tools. As an alternative you can use a nylon washer and seating set which is fitted over the valve seat.

When water trickles over the top of the tap cover it means that a leak has developed through the gland, and the tap handle should be removed. A small grub screw holds the handle to the spindle; remove this screw and put in a safe place. After removing the screw an upward tap should free the handle; a piece of wedged hardwood, inserted between the handle and cover, should free it if it sticks.

Undo the gland screw and remove the old packing. Replace this with wool, cotton wool or even string soaked in grease—such as petroleum jelly or tallow. Compress this into the stuffing box but leave enough room for the gland screw to tighten securely on its thread. Do not over-pack the stuffing box as this will make the tap hard to turn. In the event of subsequent leaks one or two extra turns on the gland screw should cure the trouble.

If the faulty tap is a 'Supatap' you are lucky, since replacing a washer on this type of tap does not necessitate turning off the water supply.

CISTERNS

Modern flushing toilet cisterns are piston actuated, unlike the older bell-type ones. The bell type of cistern can be easily recognized by its bell-like central dome; it does not normally require attention, other than possible adjustment to the ball valve. In both types of unit if the ball float becomes perforated or the washer on the outlet is faulty the cistern will overflow.

In the more efficient piston-actuated siphon, when the lever is depressed or the chain pulled a disc or plunger in the siphon dome rises. The water is forced above it, round the U-bend and down the flush pipe. A partial vacuum is created in the flush pipe, sufficient to siphon off the water remaining in the cistern. The disc is perforated to allow water to flow through it from the cistern, the holes being closed on the initial upstroke by a plastic flap or washer which acts as a non-return valve. If the washer is distorted or punctured, the flushing action may fail completely or be impaired in efficiency.

To change the washer on a piston-actuated cistern, the cistern must be flushed and the ball float arm tied up. This will shut off the flow of water. Bale out or mop up any small residue of water. Next, unlock the nut beneath the cistern which secures the flush pipe to the siphon unit. On some plastic cisterns this nut will only be hand tight. If an adjustable spanner or wrench is needed this will also be useful to undo the larger nut which holds the siphon unit to the base of the cistern.

The flush-lever linkage must then be removed. This may simply be a matter of lifting it out bodily, but arrangements may vary with different types. Next lift out the siphon, remove the plunger disc from the base of the dome and take off the small retaining washer which holds the valve washer in position. Check the size and replace it with an equivalent one. If the maker's replacement washer is not available it is possible to make a replacement part by cutting a disc of heavy PVC sheeting. You can use the old washer as a template.

The unit can now be reassembled. When replacing the siphon unit, check that the joint between it and the cistern is good. If the washer is worn, replace it and use a smear of jointing compound to ensure a watertight joint. Check carefully that the connections at the base of the cistern are satisfactory before releasing the valve arm and allowing the cistern to refill.

The procedure for repairing or replacing faulty ball valves is the same for a cold water-storage cistern or a WC. Worn washers, perforated ball floats, eroded seatings or deposits of lime or grit on moving parts are usually to blame. The operation does not involve the removal of the cistern outlet connections, but the supply to the cistern must be shut off. If replacement of the entire mechanism becomes necessary, make sure that, if the unit is correctly connected to the low-pressure (storage) supply, a similar low-pressure valve is refitted and not one of the high-pressure pattern.

109

If the ball is perforated it will become water-logged, causing the overflow to run continuously. A faulty outlet washer may lead to a similar condition. Worn valve seatings can be reground, but capping with a nylon seat or replacement of the whole unit can be affected at the cost of a few pence.

A new ball simply screws on to the threaded spindle at the end of the arm. A temporary repair can be made by draining the ball and putting it inside a polythene bag, tying the neck of the bag over the lever arm.

To replace a faulty washer, remove the cistern lid and remove the split pin which secures the lever of the ball-valve piston. The piston can then be removed. You may have on some types first to remove the cap on the end of the cylinder. Using a wrench, uncouple the washer retaining cap. The piston will then detach into two halves. If there is any grit behind the valve seating, flush it out before replacing the valve.

Noise

Noise can be caused by water turbulence. On the 'Garston' type of ball valve, the valve may be mounted on a vertical arm. Here the flow is controlled by a rubber diaphragm which operates against a nylon nozzle. To gain access, unscrew the cap at the valve end of the lever arm. A great advantage of the Garston is reduced wear on the moving parts, which are kept away from water to prevent scaling up.

AIR LOCKS

It is rare to get air locks in modern plumbing systems but they are liable to occur after refilling, repairing or alterations to a system. The most common form of air lock is when a volume of air is trapped between two bodies of water in a pipe run just before it changes direction from up to down. Mains pressure will usually provide enough force to force the air bubble to the nearest tap or ball valve, where it is released. However, the situation is more difficult where the pipe is fed from the cold-water storage cistern and there may be insufficient pressure to move the air. A method of clearing this type of air lock on the low-pressure, storage-cistern side is to connect it to the high-pressure rising-mains side. A piece of hose is used to join two taps—one end on the high and one end on the low pressure side. Leave a tap or ball-valve open on the air-locked side to allow the air to escape when both taps are turned on.

Should the air lock be on the hot-water side, temporarily block off the vent pipe above the cold-water cistern. Remember to unblock the vent once the air lock is cleared. It is wise to fit air-release locks where air locks continually occur. These can be in the form of a fitting with a venting device.

WASTE SYSTEMS

With reasonable luck, waste systems do not require much attention unless there is a specific problem. During winter months, ensure that any external waste pipes are not allowed to hold water. This may happen in horizontal runs or if the waste pipe sags.

While it is not essential to clean waste traps frequently it may be said that routine clearing will help to prevent large blockages. If you are unfortunate enough to suffer the inconvenience of a blocked waste trap, the blockage can often be cleared with the aid of a rubber plunger cup. When using the plunger, first half fill the sink or basin with water, if it is not already full. Temporarily block any overflow outlets, then work the plunger up and down over the drain hole with a jabbing motion.

If the blockage refuses to move, you will then have to remove the plug in the U-bend or undo the trap and try to hook out the obstacle. If the plug is tight, make sure the pipework is firmly supported before you attempt to undo it. Also check that you have a large container below the trap to collect the débris and water when the blockage is cleared.

It is also possible to clear blocked WC's with a plunger, but it should be used with care as there is a danger of breaking the pan.

That bugbear of cold weather, the burst pipe, is becoming a thing of the past with a greater general awareness of the need for pipe lagging and loft insulation. The burst pipe is usually an example of borrowed time; until the weather becomes warmer and the pipe thaws—and the water floods out—you do not know of the existence of the burst. For this reason it is wise, in cold weather, to check all lagging. If a pipe has burst, it will be distended and locked with ice. This is the time to mend the burst, before it thaws and floods.

First shut off the water supply, then gently heat the burst with a blow torch; keep a receptacle at hand for the thawed water to run into. It is simpler to cut out the burst with a hacksaw and rejoint the pipe. If the pipe is in lead, the jointing technique is that described in Chapter 12. Merely joint the pipe with a section of copper, preparing the ends and working as described. The only difference is that a pair of joints are made, one at each end of the short pipe section.

For copper pipe, the section should be cut out and a fitting—copper or capillary—should be used to joint the section. The technique here is that for normal pipe joining. Copper pipe is soft and resilient, and will not readily burst. Stainless steel is a much harder metal and will resist the expansion which takes place when water freezes and turns to ice. The same repair procedures apply, of course, if a pipe is holed.

Compression fittings can provide a 'safety valve', since frozen water may push off the fitting with no further harm to the pipe. Thawing out and remaking the joint is all that is necessary in such circumstances.

Finally, make sure that pipe lagging and general insulation is sound, so as to avoid a repetition. Prevention is always better than cure!

12

WIPING A LEAD JOINT

Wiping a lead joint is one of the arts of plumbing. At one time it was an essential skill for any plumbing work. With the increasing use of copper and other plumbing pipe materials, lead work is no longer the important feature it once was. However, the wiped solder joint may still be needed in situations where the domestic supply to the house is made in lead. A wiped joint will then be necessary to fit a stopcock, or a copper extension piece to which a stopcock can be joined.

Making a wiped joint involves cleaning the lead pipe and belling this out to accept a section of pipe or fitting, then building up a smooth, thick tapered fillet of solder over the joined ends. Two special tools are needed—a hardwood cone or metal 'dolly' to bell out the pipe end, and a 'mole' cloth for wiping the joint. Materials needed are tinning solder, a 450-gramme (1 lb) stick of plumber's metal, flux, a tin of plumber's black, and tallow, for use in wiping the join with the mole. The mole is also coated with tallow before it is used.

Sometimes only a short piece of incoming lead pipe may be left and care should be taken in manipulating this, since it is quite easy to fracture it and real problems of connecting may be caused. Where connections are being made to an incoming service, turn off the water at the company's stopcock in the road or at your own main stopcock if you have one.

The lead pipe must first be trimmed; a hacksaw can be used for this. Then insert the cone or dolly. The hardwood one is tapped in with a hammer. As you drive it in, twist the cone after each blow to prevent it from sticking. The metal dolly, resembling a screwdriver with a rounded tip, is rotated in the pipe with an outward pressure and motion.

Once the pipe has been belled, to a depth of about 40 mm or $1\frac{1}{2}$ in, apply plumber's black for about another 50 mm. The purpose of this is to stop solder from spreading beyond the limits of the joint. The completed joint will be about 75

1

2

3

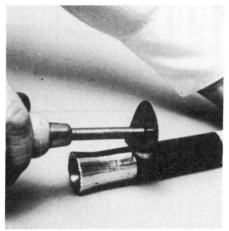

4

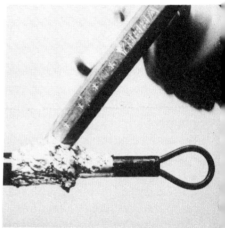

5

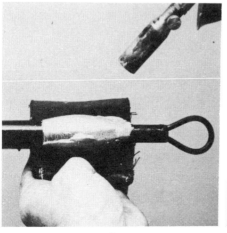

6

7

mm (3 in) long. The receiving pipe, or spigot of the fitting should be similarly treated.

Using a shavehook or a penknife clean the end and the inside of the pipe. Scrape the outside until the metal is bright, up to the line of the plumber's black. Fine wire wool should be used to clean the fitting or spigot. The end of the fitting or pipe should be slightly bevelled to facilitate a good fit. A file can be used for this.

To solder, coat both ends evenly with flux. The two ends are then brought firmly together and the whole area of the joint is heated with a blow torch. Keep the flame moving to ensure even distribution of heat. Heat the joint just sufficiently to melt the solder and then tin both surfaces. The plumber's metal is then applied to the joint. Fill the rim of the belled portion. Apply only sufficient heat to melt the solder to a plastic consistency, so that it does not run off the joint.

Use about a quarter of a stick of solder and then heat the mole in the flame and dip it in tallow. Use a circular wiping motion to spread the solder around the joint, tapering to the ends of the joint. You will need to reheat the solder mildly and carefully from time to time, to keep it workable. Build up the solder until you have used about three-quarters of the stick and then reheat and wipe the joint smooth with neatly faired edges.

Allow the joint to cool before in any way disturbing it. Take great care to avoid manipulating the pipe while making the joint as it may fracture.

Wiping a lead joint

1. A file is used to smooth the cut end of the pipe

2. Plumber's black is applied over the joint to prevent the solder metal from spreading beyond limits

3. Wooden 'dolly', or cone, being used to bell out the end of the pipe

4. A shave hook used to clean up the area of pipe to be coated with plumber's mental; this area is next tinned with solder

5. A layer of plumber's metal is built up evenly around the pipe. The loop is a piece of spring metal inserted in the copper tube to facilitate inserting into the lead and for controlling the pipe during lead wiping

6. The mole, dipped in tallow, is used to wipe the metal around the joint, feathering the edges

7. A neat, wiped joint with fitting connected to the copper end

13

SEPTIC DRAINAGE AND CESSPOOLS

Main drainage is not available in many rural areas and individual and, in some cases, group sewage-disposal or collection methods are used, known respectively as septic tanks and cesspools.

The cesspool is a storage tank, set below ground, which has to be emptied periodically by the local authority. This must be completely watertight, as there can be no seepage to the surrounding soil. The sides and bottom must be at least 150 mm thick. A strong cement-mortar (1 : 3) mix, containing a waterproofing agent, should be used as a lining for brickwork or other construction.

Sewage is extremely noxious, and ventilation must be provided to vent the gases. Ideally, the cesspool should be sited as far away from the house as possible. It should have a minimum capacity of 18 183 litres (4,000 gallons), measured from below the inlet level. A strong cover must be provided—this is usually made of concrete—and an access hatch must also be fitted to allow for inspection.

Nevertheless, the cesspool is less desirable than the septic tank and only used normally where impervious sub-soil renders the situation unsuitable for septic drainage through the soakaway. The septic tank breaks down solid sewage into liquid form by means of bacterial action. The harmful elements are filtered off and the residual liquid is then drained into a soakaway pit.

The tank consists of two chambers, with sewage entering the first chamber through a dip pipe which ensures that the scum forming on the surface is not disturbed. Sludge falls to the bottom and the remainder breaks up into liquid form in the chamber. This then goes through another dip pipe into the second chamber. Then it passes through a filter where a distribution plate normally spreads the liquid over the entire filter bed. Once filtering is complete, the liquid passes out near the bottom of the tank to the soakaway.

In the first, or settlement chamber, primary sewage purification is carried out by anaerobes—micro-organisms living and breathing without need of oxygen from the atmosphere. These organisms help to break up the solids. The partially digested sludge which falls to the bottom must be removed periodically by a tanker. If this is not done, eventual breakdown of the anaerobe process occurs. A minimum of 27 300 litres (600 gallons) is laid down for the settlement chambers of septic tanks.

A biological filter in the second chamber, over which the effluent passes, completes the treatment. The filter should be crush resistant against its own weight and roughly cubicle in shape. Among suitable filter materials are hand-broken stone, washed quartzite gravel and hard burnt clinker. Filter material must be carefully graded. The bottom layer may consist of large pieces of 100 mm to 150 mm in size, laid to a depth of 150 mm. Finer material, capable of passing through a 25 mm to 50 mm gauge mesh, is laid on to this. The overall depth of the filter should not be less than 760 mm to 1 m.

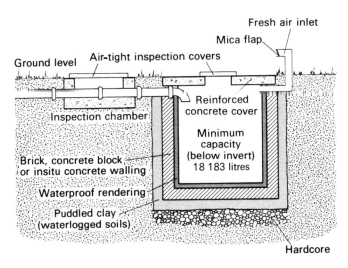

Scheme for septic-tank drainage

117

An organic film, forming on the filter material, oxidizes most of the remaining polluted matter. The process is the work of aerobes, which thrive only in the presence of atmospheric oxygen, unlike anaerobes. To supply oxygen it is necessary to provide ventilation, and this is done by means of a vent pipe which terminates at the base of the filter chamber. More sophisticated septic tanks provide for half-round channels with open joints under the filter material. This helps to prevent the build-up of liquids in the chamber.

The soakaway pit, the usual method of final disposal, should be lined where conditions of very soft soil exist. Walls can be built of bricks or concrete blocks, and poured concrete can be used, though this involves a considerable amount of timber shuttering. Concrete should be composed of not less than 1 : 2 : 4, cement, sand and coarse aggregate. Wall thickness should be between 150 mm and 230 mm thick, dependent on the soil of the locality. The walls should be made impervious with a sand-and-cement rendering, finished off to a smooth surface with a steel trowel.

Inlet pipes to both cesspools and septic tanks should be interrupted by an inspection chamber or an interceptor fitting. This provides access for inspection and cleaning. The inlet pipe, after entering the tank, is terminated with a T-fitting which acts as a 'dip pipe' and slows down inflowing sewage. This enters the tank vertically and below the surface of the contents, avoiding turbulence and promoting settlement of sludge.

The outflow pipe on septic tanks should be about 50 mm lower than the inlet. The arrangement of the dip pipe also helps prevent blockage of outlet and inlet points by any deposits floating on the surface.

Tanks can be either square, rectangular or round. Cesspools are usually square and septic tanks rectangular, the latter generally being three times as long as they are wide. Round tanks are usually built from prefabricated concrete 'kits'. Covers can be of reinforced concrete, pre-cast panels, or steel plates. Temporary shuttering, wood or galvanized-iron, can be used for in-situ casting of concrete covers.

TESTING

Local authority testing is carried out and a tank will be expected to hold a full load of water for 24 hours without a fall in level of more than 25 mm. The tank should be filled about 24 hours before testing, to allow for surface absorption, and then topped up for the test.

14

RAINWATER SERVICES

Usually, rainwater goods are made either of cast iron or plastic. As stated in Chapter 9, it is possible to join plastic to cast iron by means of adaptors. Zinc and asbestos are other types of guttering but these are little used compared with cast iron and plastic. Asbestos tends to become brittle with age. Guttering is also made in pressed steel, usually supplied galvanized or primed, and vitreous enamel, available in a wide range of colours.

Worn and damaged cast-iron guttering can be repaired up to a point, but it is often advisable to replace it. Much depends, of course, on the state of disrepair or damage—a leaking pipe may saturate a wall and can cause immense damage to the fabric of the house; plaster can be affected and may have to be replaced; wood can rot and furniture and fitments can all suffer.

Not only damaged pipes can cause problems. Blocked guttering may cause overflowing to occur, and the spillage, particularly during periods of heavy rainfall, may do instant damage. To guard against all these problems, guttering should be regularly inspected and maintained. Spring and autumn are good times for inspection and any necessary attention—on the first occasion to remove any accumulation of leaves deposited during the winter, which may clog pipes and guttering, and again in the autumn in preparation for the wet winter weather.

For maintenance, a few, simple home-made tools will suffice. A home-made scraper, resembling a garden hoe, with the 'business end' fashioned to fit the contour of the guttering, can be made from a piece of hardboard fixed to a short handle. Down pipes can be unblocked by using a rag firmly bound to a cane as a plunger. Make sure that the rag is well secured, since if it comes adrift it may create a further blockage.

Before unblocking a down pipe, careful inspection should

be made to try to establish the cause. It may be advisable, if the blockage resists clearance and appears extensive, to uncouple the section of pipe, as you may otherwise transfer the cause of the blockage to a less accessible point in the system.

Blockages in an angled pipe may usually be cleared by prodding the point of blockage with a piece of stiff wire. Take care, with plastic in particular, that you do not damage the pipe. Prevention is always better than cure, and blockages to down pipes can usually be prevented by using a proprietary guard over the mouth of the pipe or by crumpling a piece of chicken wire and using this as a guard. Wire guards are also made which cover long areas of guttering.

One cause of leakage may be sagging brackets, causing joints to come apart. Brackets may need replacement or may merely be loose. Before replacing these or tightening loose fixings, check the joints. These may need recaulking on metal pipe and plastic seals may have deteriorated on plastic pipes. On other types of pipe, new mastic joints may be needed.

With half-round gutters, special repair brackets can be bought which fix to the fascia board and enable the guttering to be secured without the need for removal. When refixing old brackets, check the screw holes; these may have become damaged and enlarged. Replug them with wood, plastic, fibre or aluminium plugs, otherwise sagging may recur.

Cast-iron guttering pipe is bolted together in sections, with a sealant between the joints. This is usually a mastic or putty and red lead. If the nut and bolt are rusted and resist all attempts to free them with penetrating oil, the nut should simply be cut off with a hacksaw and replaced with a new nut and bolt. New seals can then be made.

Rusted pipe in no great state of deterioration can be thoroughly wire brushed, treated with an anti-rust liquid, cleaned out and given two coats of a bitumastic paint. Another method of repair can be carried out with glass fibre, in the form of resin-bonded glass-fibre mat or padding; there are various makes of glass-fibre kit on the market. Again, the pipework should first be thoroughly wire brushed and cleaned out before you make the repair. Rust on the back of

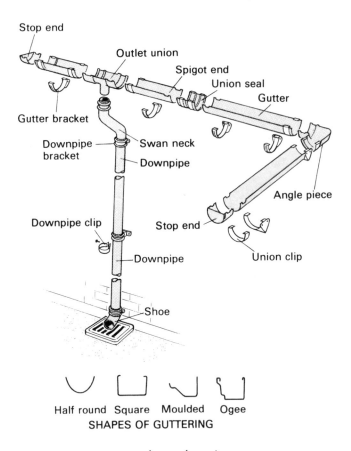

Stop end

Outlet union

Spigot end

Union seal

Gutter

Gutter bracket

Downpipe bracket

Swan neck

Downpipe

Angle piece

Downpipe clip

Stop end

Downpipe

Union clip

Shoe

Half round Square Moulded Ogee

SHAPES OF GUTTERING

above and opposite

The layout for cast-iron and plastic guttering is similar. The hopper head, shown
with the plastic guttering is used to receive waste water from bath and
wash basin

ogee cast-iron pipe is more easily treated if the pipework is
dismantled. The shape of this pipe may preclude your getting
completely to the back of the pipe with it fixed in position.

The erection of new guttering is not complicated, but you
will need assistance if you opt for cast iron. Guttering over
porches and the like can be put up with the help of trestles
and scaffold planks. It is very important that you are on a
level with the gutter position, otherwise you will find it difficult to line up the guttering correctly.

Where guttering is being fitted or replaced at roof level,

122

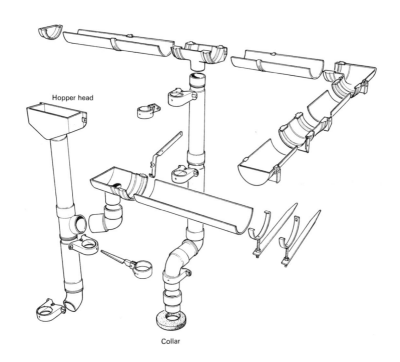

Hopper head

Collar

you will need scaffolding. A portable scaffold tower is the best arrangement. This is easy to erect and can be mounted on wheels, so that it can be easily positioned where it is wanted. Avoid working on a ladder. If it is necessary to be able to work over a longer distance than afforded by a tower, two of these can be used, at each end of the working area, bridged by timber scaffold staging, which consists of long, substantial planks. Towers can be hired and enable the job to be tackled more safely and with greater efficiency.

The terminology of rainwater goods is not extensive, and the main descriptions are as follows: gutter—section collecting the storm water; down pipe—means of draining the accumulated water; stop end—section at end of run of gutter; running outlet—intermediate termination with spigot to connect gutter and down pipe; hopper head—a connector fed by individual pipes and connected to a down pipe; swanneck —an angled section which provides a stand-off where the fascia, to which the guttering fixes, is forward of the line of the wall; shoe—an angled outlet at the bottom of the down

123

pipe, used where water discharges over a trapped yard gully; angles—sections, like a short letter 'L', for inside and outside angles: these are made in 90°, 120° and 135° angles, dependent on manufacturer. Stop ends can be combined with outlets, and there are also long and short stop ends. There are a variety of other fittings and connectors for more specialized purposes, such as PVC to cast-iron connectors.

It is a good idea to obtain a catalogue of rainwater goods from a given manufacturer; while fixing techniques do not vary greatly, there are variations between the different firms. This will also enable you to identify the parts you need for your individual situation.

Guttering is available in various different patterns. Plastic guttering is either a half-round or a square section. The latter has, in fact, a greater water-carrying capacity than the half-round type. Two other types of pipe are the cast-iron 'ogee' section, which is a cross between half-round and square sec-

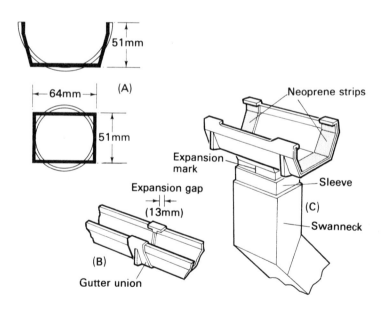

(A) Comparison of water-carrying capacity of round and rectangular guttering

(B) Gap must be left for thermal expansion on PVC guttering

(C) Component parts of a rainwater outlet

tion, and the moulded section. Where you opt for cast-iron pipe you will need help because of its weight: fixing plastic rainwater goods can be done single-handedly.

ERECTING A PLASTIC RAINWATER SYSTEM

Plastic rainwater goods are the best and quickest choice for the average handyman, and usually require no maintenance or repainting. The following description of the fitting of a complete new rainwater service is of a PVC system.

Plastic guttering is usually available in grey, white and black, but not necessarily in both half round and square in all these colours. Before starting work, estimate the amount of guttering you need. Plastic guttering is made in 4 m lengths, and pipe is available in sizes from 2.5 m to 4 m. You will need to determine where outlets and down pipes must be fitted in relation to drainage arrangements. Once you have measured for the run of guttering and down pipe, you can then fill in the requirements for connectors, stop ends, shoes, swannecks and the like. Most guttering section is lapped together, in neoprene seals secured with clips, to form a 'dry' joint. Some makes use a union—a short section with neoprene seals at each end—into which the gutter sections are located. Other systems employ variations in the methods of securing sections of guttering or in the type of down-pipe fixing. Broadly, the methods are similar and these variations are only of detail. Some forms of plastic guttering, but not down pipes, are cement welded. Where existing neoprene seals have deteriorated in existing plastic guttering these can be replaced.

It is quite a good idea to set up sections on the ground before assembly to make sure that you have all the parts and that they fit together correctly for the given situation.

The fixing brackets have to be screwed into place and must be lined up as described below. They can generally be fixed to the fascia board which is fitted below the eaves of most houses. However, in some situations a different type of bracket called a rafter side bracket may be needed.

Guttering should be secured at a maximum of 1 m centres (about 3 ft). Start at one end and work along progressively

125

when fixing the brackets, which are secured with non-rusting screws. Your outlet sockets have to line up accurately with the ground connections or outlets and this should be checked most carefully before you proceed.

There must be a slight fall in the guttering to carry the volume of water away to the down-pipe outlet, otherwise you could face the possibility of an overflow during periods of heavy rainfall. The outlet is at the lowest point and the fall should be even, to avoid collection of water at any other point. To ensure this, a string line should be used to locate the brackets. A thin nylon string is suitable.

Temporarily fix a nail into the fascia at one end and attach the string to this. Fix a nail at a point corresponding to the end of that run of guttering and secure the end of the line to this. Use a spirit level to make sure that the line is level.

The fall in the guttering is usually a ratio of 1 : 40. This has to be consistent to the point of outlet, so that there is no distortion of guttering through misalignment of brackets. Establish the degree of fall—that is one fortieth of the total distance. Next, measure this amount below the temporary nail which represents the far end, or outflow point, of the guttering. Reset the string line to this lower position and you will have the correct fall.

The string should be taut and not sag. Set the brackets to line up exactly on the string line and screw them to the fascia.

When joining sections of guttering together, allow 13 mm for expansion between each section. There is usually an expansion mark indicated on the joints. Once sections are in position, the joints are usually secured by clips, which clamp the seal tight to ensure a leak-free union. On some makes a notching tool has to be employed as the clips are recessed into the top edge of the guttering. These tools can usually be hired or bought cheaply.

Guttering and down pipe are both easily cut with a fine-tooth saw. Do not cut at the ends with the seals. Cuts should be made squarely, so that guttering and pipe are accurately aligned and seated, otherwise the seal may not be effective. With square sectioning, it is not difficult to cut the pipe and guttering accurately, as a try-square can be used. In the case of half-round guttering, newspaper can be used as a template, wrapped round the pipe at the intended cut position, with the corners in line. A section of guttering can also be used as a template.

It cannot be emphasized too strongly that measurements must be taken most carefully before cutting—and these should be rechecked. Errors can cause frustration and the waste of both time and relatively expensive material.

Brackets should not usually be located further than 150 mm (6 in) away from a socket. Stop ends, which may incorporate the socket outlet, can be put on latterly. Angle pieces are simply reversed to give a choice of an inside or an outside angle, and clipped similarly to a run of straight guttering. Usually, the 90° section is required at angles. You can check the angle by making a card or hardboard template.

Down pipes must be fixed at a maximum of 2 m (78 in) centres, joined by a socket spigot connector. This allows for expansion upwards over the spigot. In some situations, a spacer may be needed between these joints. Down pipes must also be lined up accurately with the outlet at ground level. This may be a direct connection to drainage or a soakaway, or a shoe may be fitted to discharge into a trapped yard gulley.

Lining up is done by means of a plumb bob—a weight on a length of string. This is centred through the outlet and carefully lined up. Adjustments should be made, if need be, to the positioning of the outlet on the guttering, since distortion to the down pipe must be avoided. Mark the vertical alignment at intervals on the wall with chalk, which can be easily brushed off, and use this to establish the fixing points for the fixing brackets.

It is a good idea, where possible, to make the fixings into the mortar joints between brickwork. A masonry drill can be used to drill the brickwork, which should be plugged for screw fixing; the screws should be of the non-rusting variety. Alternatively, masonry nails can be used. These do not need wall plugging as for screw fixings. The type of fixing will depend on the surface; usually three lengths of nail and screw are available to meet the needs for various penetrations.

Check finally that joints are able to expand to the extent prescribed.

Connections to below-ground services are made in accordance with the nature of the service—glazed, pitch-fibre or plastic pipe, as described earlier. In the case of discharge over a gulley, the shoe fitting is simply attached.

DRAINAGE

Drainage may be to a sump or soakaway, into main soil systems, or into highway stormwater sewers. Drainage into main sewers is not usually permitted and frequently drainage via stormwater sewers is disapproved of. This is because it would be easy to overload these services in periods of very heavy rainfall. Instead, the soakaway is the preferred method of rainwater disposal. This is eventually tapped by the local water company as the water collects at the water level or 'table' for the locality, and can be utilized, after treatment, for domestic distribution.

The size of soakaway pit depends on the amount of stormwater capacity. Generally, a pit, some 460 $1.812m^3$ (64 cu ft)/mm (18 in) below ground level, with a concrete lid and the pit lined with selected hardcore (rubble), will disperse the water. If the soil is excessively friable, a brick chamber may have to be constructed, so that the sides do not cave in. As an alternative, the soakaway can be filled with a random honeycomb of bricks.

The pipe from the stormwater drainage is taken into the soakaway at about one third of the way up from the bottom and about one third of the way in. The pipe should enter the soakaway with a slight downward slope.